UNIVERSITY
OF WISCONSIN
BASKETBALL

National champs! The University of Wisconsin–Madison (UW) basketball team celebrates its 1941 NCAA championship victory by carrying coach Harold "Bud" Foster off the court.

On the front cover: Please see page 102. (Courtesy University of Wisconsin Digital Collections and Arcvies.)

On the back cover: Please see page 78. (Courtesy University of Wisconsin Digital Collections and Arcvies.)

Cover background: Please see page 77. (Courtesy University of Wisconsin Digital Collections and Arcvies.)

UNIVERSITY OF WISCONSIN BASKETBALL

Dave Anderson

ARCADIA
PUBLISHING

Published by Arcadia Publishing
Charleston, South Carolina

Library of Congress Catalog Card Number: 2006931412

For all general information contact Arcadia Publishing at:
Telephone 843-853-2070
Fax 843-853-0044
E-mail sales@arcadiapublishing.com
For customer service and orders:
Toll-Free 1-888-313-2665

Visit us on the Internet at www.arcadiapublishing.com

*Dedicated to two very strong people who persevered
through tremendous physical challenges during the writing of this book.
My wife, Maureen, and my brother Paul.
All the very best.
And to my father, thank you.*

CONTENTS

ACKNOWLEDGMENTS

Many thanks to the Board of Regents of the University of Wisconsin System for use of all the great images displayed in this book.

And many thanks go to these three fine people at the University of Wisconsin–Madison: university archivists David Null and Bernie Schermetzler and university communications specialist Jeff Miller. All three are gentlemen and scholars who provided tremendous help with my research to find the historic images featured within this volume.

I also wish to acknowledge the players and coaches of the 1976 UW Cancer Research intramural basketball team. Thanks for letting me play. We almost won it all.

INTRODUCTION

As a Wisconsin native and a graduate of the University of Wisconsin–Madison (UW), I thought I was a knowledgeable fan and follower of Badger athletics. Boy was I wrong. While doing research for this book, I discovered something I never knew: UW owns one of the greatest basketball programs in the history of college sports.

There, I said it.

Right now, picking yourself up off the floor, you might be angry or amused. If it is the former, you are no doubt a fan of another college hoops team and are quickly rattling off all the other schools you believe are better. So for the point of argument, why not fall into the latter group—thank you for your open mind—and at least say, well, UW has had a fairly good program and produced some fine players in recent memory, but what about the early days? Now, dear reader, this is where I have you, because the early days for UW basketball date back to 1898. And a lot of truly great and wonderful things have happened with Badger basketball since that long-ago year.

Let's start at the very beginning.

The first public game of basketball took place in Springfield, Massachusetts, on March 1, 1892, and made its way just over 1,000 miles west to officially become a men's school sport at UW in 1898. After getting its feet wet by going 0-3 in the initial season (stay with me now), UW commenced to post one winning season after another (with the only exception being 8-9 in 1905), never again having a losing year until 1919 when the team fell to 5-11. Then the Badgers quickly righted the ship. They went 15-5 the next season and stayed the course as winners. The mountain of wins they had piled up in the first two decades grew even more in the 1920s as their collegiate hoops domination continued. The highlights during these 41 spectacular winning years were many. UW basketball excelled at home in Madison and across the country. I call 1900 to 1941 the "First Golden Era" for UW basketball. I have many reasons.

Take, for example, the Badger teams of 1902–1905 featuring Christian Steinmetz. Called "the father of Wisconsin basketball," Steinmetz was a dramatic scorer who became UW's first All-American. In 1904–1905, Steinmetz scored 462 points over 18 games (at more than 25 points a game, that was more than most teams' total four-quarter production during this era) and led the Badgers to their first national title game. Steinmetz is not only a charter inductee of the UW Athletic Hall of Fame but is a member of the National Basketball Hall of Fame.

Enter player-coach Emmett Angell. His versatility and success has never been duplicated in collegiate basketball. Angell coached the 1904–1908 Badger squads to a record of 43-15, tying for first place his last two seasons in the newly formed Big Ten Conference. As a player, he put up 96 points in his first year on the court and led the Badgers to a 12-2 record. One of the best coaches during the early days of basketball in America was UW's Dr. Walter E. "Doc" Meanwell. Between 1906 and 1929, Meanwell's Badger teams won 12 Big Ten titles (Missouri stole him away to coach 1917–1921, but he returned to UW for the 1920–1921 season and conference title). In 1912 and 1914, UW won Big Ten and national titles. Meanwell's overall coaching record with the Badgers was 246-99-1.

During this First Golden Era, covering 41 years, UW was a scoring machine but maintained an amazing defense. In a game on January 6, 1914, in Madison, UW blanked Parsons College 50-0. It was then and will undoubtedly always be the only shutout in Big Ten basketball history.

By now, if I have not won you over, at least admit I am making a case that Badger basketball history stands with the best of them. And we have not yet gotten out of the 1920s! Working up to the 1940s, the 1940–1941 campaign was a truly special season when UW won the NCAA Basketball championship. UW advanced through the NCAA bracket, defeating Dartmouth College 51-50 and the University of Pittsburgh 36-30, to get into the national title game in Kansas City, Missouri, where it beat Washington State 39-34. This famous Badger team was led by National Basketball Hall of Fame coach Harold "Bud" Foster and All-America players John Kotz and Gene Englund.

Overall, admittedly, things slowed down more than a bit for UW basketball during the middle of the 20th century before picking up and evolving into one of the top NCAA programs in the country. But I say "overall" because within this quiet period there still were, like discovering diamonds in the rough, exciting players, top coaches, and occasional, wonderful successes. I call this time "in between the Golden Eras." Then, in the 1990s and into this century, Badger basketball recaptured its winning ways, just like in those early days. This achievement is why I refer to the period from 1993 to the present as the "Second Golden Era."

All of the time men were playing basketball at UW, women were as well. Actually, one of the photographs in this book shows a Badger women's hoops competition in 1897, but it would not be until 1974 that they could play on an intercollegiate level. Add their program into this book (which I am honored to do) and I am really making a strong case, because the UW women's basketball program has evolved into one of the strongest and most popular in the country.

This volume describes in detail and shows historic images of the many great Badger players, coaches, and teams through it all. I hope after reading it, you, like me, will see and enjoy the big picture, discover a newfound appreciation for Badger hoops history, and say this is one of the greatest basketball programs in the history of college sports.

1

THE FIRST GOLDEN ERA

My home is in New Hampshire now, but Wisconsin—known as America's Dairyland—is where I lived for my initial 22 years. Yes there are a good number of cows there, but also many other wonderful attractions and equally wonderful people. If you have been there, you know what I mean. I was excited about traveling there to get research started on this book. Quite honestly, I was not sure what I would find in the archives about Badger hoops history, but at least, I told myself, I should have a good time. Following business in Chicago, I hopped in my well-equipped rental car (silver Taurus with acrylic carpeting, tinted glass, and AM/FM) and jetted north out of Illinois and into the diminishing Wisconsin twilight. I forged northwest under platinum clouds with just a subtle sunset the color of sharp cheddar, made great time despite the billboard temptations, and a couple hours later made it to Madison, state capital and home to the University of Wisconsin–Madison (UW).

First thing the next morning I parked in a garage off State Street, attempting to be as close as possible to Memorial Library. It was raining with a brisk wind, but alas, the calendar said May so many a coed walked around in shorts nonetheless. My first appointment was with UW archivist David Null. I picked up a pass at the main desk and, after getting lost for a few minutes, found my way to his office on Memorial Library's lower level. It was—as Yogi Berra would say—"déjà vu all over again," because just a year earlier I had been in David's office to conduct research for my book *University of Wisconsin Football*. Just as they had been before, David and his coworkers were extremely helpful, providing boxes of dusty stored materials. I dug in, starting at the beginning in 1898, and the more I read the more astonished I became.

Over the next several hours, I discovered one winning team after another. I did a bit of math and figured that during the first three decades of the 20th century UW's basketball teams had compiled a record of 331-117—a truly impressive winning percentage of .739. In retrospect, it is reasonably understandable why people would not know about this domination of Badger basketball across the country. Not only was it a long time ago, but basketball truly was in its infancy then; for example, the game would not be played at the Olympics until 1936 in Berlin (interesting side note: the United States won the gold medal and James Naismith, the founder of the game in 1892, was in attendance).

After the research went so extremely well at Memorial, I headed next to the fourth floor of Steenbock Library to see archivist Bernie Schermetzler. Bernie offered me access to boxes upon boxes of black-and-white photographs and transparencies. Donning white gloves, I started the search process. In no time I was overwhelmingly pleased to locate a large array of magnificent visuals to complement the morning's work at Memorial. Images revealed the teams, the famous players, the 1941 NCAA championship, the Red Gym, game action, the UW Field House. Amazed and enthused at what I was finding, I looked up into the Steenbock quiet, which seemed even more serene due to the dull, wet weather outside, and wanted to scream with joy, but did not, which was probably a good thing.

Before leaving Madison, I quickly drove around campus to see my old apartments on Broom and off Langdon on Terrace, and remarkably found a parking spot to walk around my sophomore-year dorm, Sellery Hall, for a few minutes. Even after all the years, these locations look much the same. So much are they locked in time that while driving out of town, I imagined I saw behind the Broom Street apartment my friend Fred's extra-large gold basketball shorts from our 1976 intramural team still flapping on the clothesline.

Unlike Fred's trunks, gold is a color symbolizing the very best. The First Golden Era of UW basketball certainly was that. I hope you enjoy, on the following pages, the images and information from this magnificent time.

The 1903 UW basketball team finished the season with five wins and two losses. Players scored a total of 208 points in those seven games, holding the competition to just 138. The team was led by Christian Steinmetz, pictured above holding the basketball.

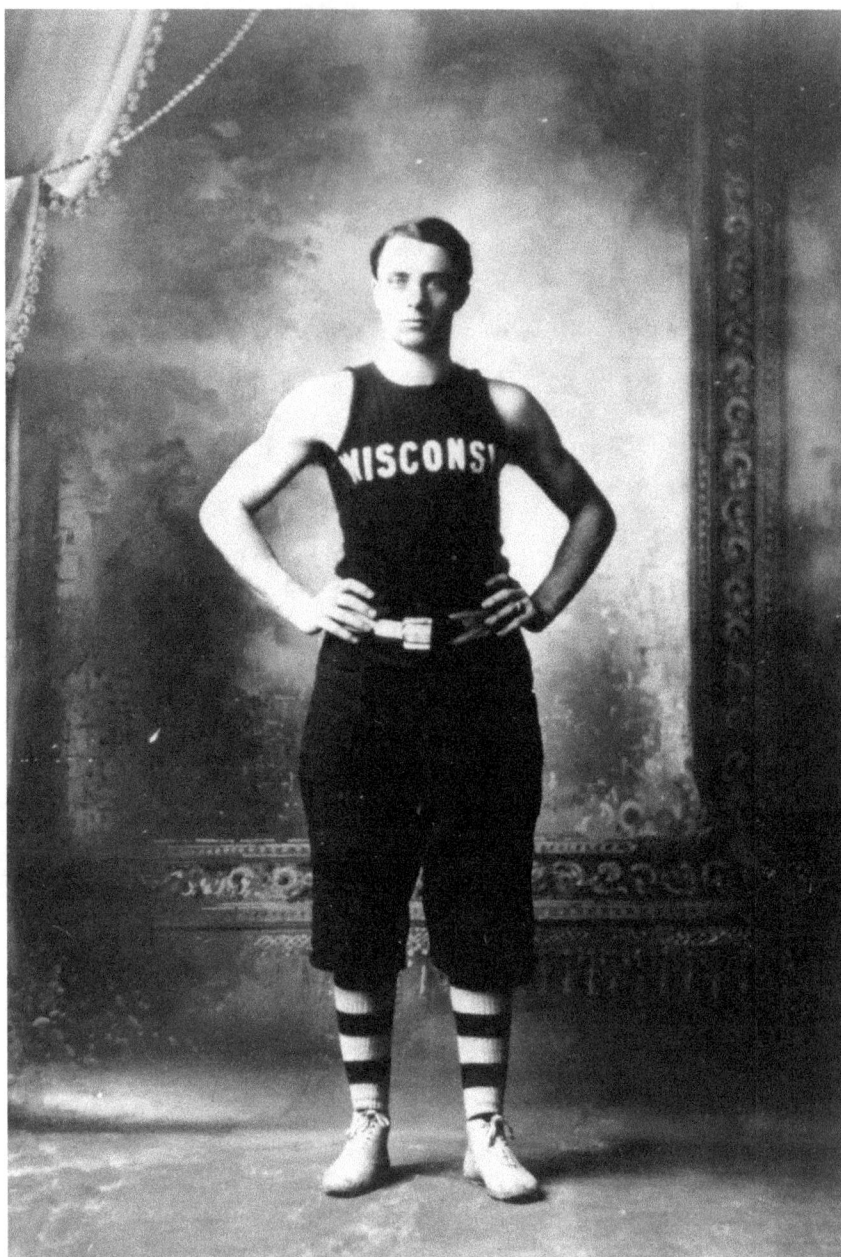

Christian Steinmetz of Milwaukee was UW's first All-American in basketball. He played from 1902 to 1905 and was a tremendous scorer, accounting for 50 of the points in a UW 75-10 victory over Company G in Sparta, Wisconsin, in 1904. During the same season, against the Two Rivers Athletic Club, he made all of UW's 26 free throws in the game (up until 1924, the rules of basketball allowed a coach to pick one player to shoot all of the free throws awarded to his team). In 1904–1905, Steinmetz set a UW single season record by scoring 462 points. His induction into the National Basketball Hall of Fame took place in 1961, and he passed away on June 11, 1963.

The 1904–1905 Badger team ended 10-3 on the season and won the Western Championship, the school's first basketball title. UW beat previously undefeated Chicago University in the championship game by a score of 29 to 24. This was the first team coached by Emmett Angell, pictured above in the top right. Angell came to UW as a gymnasium instructor and served as basketball head coach through 1908. His teams compiled an overall record of 43-15 for a winning percentage of .741, best to date in UW basketball history.

UW tied for the Big Ten title in 1907. The 1906–1907 team finished with an overall record of 11-3 and a conference game record of 6-2. For the season, the Badgers scored a total of 407 points and allowed only 264. One of the star players on this squad was forward Harlan Bethune "Biddy" Rogers, seated far right in the first row. In addition to basketball, Rogers also played football and baseball while at UW, earning nine letters. He is a member of the Wisconsin State Hall of Fame and the UW Athletic Hall of Fame.

"BIDDY" ROGERS

Harlan Bethune "Biddy" Rogers came from Portage to star at UW in three sports. In basketball, he played on the 1907 and 1908 teams, which each won a share of the Big Ten title, and served as captain for the latter squad. The Harlan B. Rogers Scholarship was established in recognition of his excellent collegiate career.

THE FIRST GOLDEN ERA

The 1911–1912 UW basketball players won all 15 games on their schedule, winning not only the conference but being named national champions by the Helms Athletic Foundation.

Otto Stangel played for the undefeated 1911–1912 Badger basketball team. He led the Big Ten in scoring that year with 177 points, a record that would stand for eight more seasons. A native of Two Rivers, Stangel was inducted into the UW Athletic Hall of Fame in 1995.

　　　　　　　　　　　　　　　　　　THE FIRST GOLDEN ERA

Brown	Diggle		Sands		Van Gent		Lange		Harper		Voss
	Anderson		Steltz		Stangel		Meanwell		Haas		
Bellows					Booth						Stephenson

The 1913–1914 squad won 15 games without a loss to capture the Big Ten title and once again be named national champions. This was UW's second national crown in three years as it dominated America's collegiate basketball scene. One game during this remarkable season was a 50-0 win over Parsons College on January 6, 1914. It is still the only shutout ever recorded in Big Ten basketball history. Coach Dr. Walter E. "Doc" Meanwell, wearing a bow tie, is seated in the second row, second from the right. Meanwell had started coaching UW basketball in 1911, and by this time his teams' win-loss record was an astounding 44-1.

This photograph of UW basketball head coach Doc Meanwell was taken in 1912. A native of Leeds, England, who graduated with a medical degree from the University of Maryland in 1909, Meanwell initially came to UW in 1911 to be a wrestling coach. But basketball was where he excelled, as his teams won Big Ten conference championships in 1912, 1913, 1914, 1916, 1921, 1923, 1924, and 1929. In 1912, 1914, and 1916, his squads posted undefeated seasons as well and were named national champions by the Helms Athletic Foundation. From 1917 to 1920, he coached at the University of Missouri, where he was also successful, winning two conference titles in three seasons before returning to Wisconsin. UW enjoyed a 246-99-1 overall record when he was head coach. Meanwell was inducted into the UW Athletic Hall of Fame in 1991 and also became a member of the National Basketball Hall of Fame.

THE FIRST GOLDEN ERA

Ruder	Levis	Chandler	Carlson	McIntosh	Morris	
		Simpson		Olsen		Meanwell
	Meyers		Hass		Smith	

The 1915–1916 Badgers continued UW's national basketball dominance, once again being named champions by the Helms Athletic Foundation. This was UW's third national title in five seasons. The 1915–1916 squad won the Big Ten with a conference record of 11-1. The overall record was 20-1. The team featured many star players, including All-American George Levis, pictured on the far left in the third row. Harold Olsen, sitting second from the right in the second row (next to coach Meanwell), would go on to serve as head coach of Ohio State University for 24 seasons, leading his teams to an overall record of 265-81. A native of Rice Lake, Olsen would also help in 1939 to create the NCAA postseason tournament now known as March Madness.

UW forward George Levis earned first-team All–Big Ten honors in 1915 and 1916, in addition to being named All-American in 1916. A Madison native, Levis continued to contribute to the game of basketball after playing at UW. He coached at the University of Indiana for two seasons and later helped to create glass backboards at his family's company, Illinois Glass.

The 1917–1918 basketball team at UW posted a 14-3 overall record and won the Big Ten title by going 9-3 in conference play. This squad was coached by Guy Lowman, seen at the far right of the second row. Lowman held his position with the Badgers basketball program for three seasons until Doc Meanwell returned in 1920. Lowman also coached football and baseball at UW and oversaw the university's department of physical education for 26 years until he passed away in 1943 at age 66. UW's baseball field on Walnut Avenue was named for him in 1952.

In the 1920–1921 basketball season, UW went 13-4 and tied for the Big Ten championship by ending at 8-4 in the conference. This season marked the return of head coach Doc Meanwell, pictured at the far right in the first row. Meanwell would continue coaching Badger basketball until 1932 and then serve as UW athletic director through 1935.

The 1922–1923 unit finished the season with a win-loss record of 12-3, scoring a total of 344 points while holding its opponents to just 198. The Badgers tied for a share of the Big Ten title with an 11-1 conference record. The team featured Rollie Williams, seen in the first row, third from left. Next to him, captain Gus Tebell holds the basketball. Williams, a native of Edgerton, also starred on the football and baseball teams, earning nine letters while at UW. He achieved All–Big Ten recognition both as a basketball guard and a football halfback. After graduation, he coached basketball at Millikin University and the University of Iowa. He was named to the UW Athletic Hall of Fame in 1991.

The Badger hoops squad of 1923–1924 earned a share of the Big Ten title with a conference win-loss record of 8-4. The players' overall record for the season was 12-4 as they scored 426 points and held their opponents to just 350. They also tied a game versus DePauw University with the score of 25-25 when it was halted after three overtimes.

The UW team of 1928–1929 also tied for the Big Ten title by winning 10 games and losing only 2 in conference play. For the season, the Badgers were 15-2, outscoring their opponents 539 points to 386. Harold E. "Bud" Foster, pictured in the middle of the second row, was named All–Big Ten as center in 1929 and 1930. Foster also earned All-America honors in 1930. After a professional stint with the Oshkosh All-Stars, he returned to coach the Badger freshman basketball team in 1933. In 1934, he became UW's head basketball coach and remained in that position for 25 years. In 1940–1941, Foster coached the UW team to the NCAA championship, where it beat Washington State 39-34 for the crown.

Bud Foster is seen here during his playing days at UW, before becoming the Badgers head coach in 1934. Foster was awarded All-America honors as the nation's top collegiate center in 1930. He is in the National Basketball Hall of Fame and was a charter inductee into the UW Athletic Hall of Fame in 1991.

The Badgers continued their winning ways during the 1929–1930 campaign with a 15-2 season record. The two losses, however, were in Big Ten competition, so the Badgers dropped to conference runners-up. This team would be the last to play its home basketball season in the Red Gym on Langdon Street in Madison. The first game in the UW Field House took place on December 18, 1930. This photograph of the 1929–1930 team was printed in the game's UW Field House dedication program. The first three decades of the 20th century truly were tremendously successful for UW's basketball teams, as they compiled a record of 331-117, an impressive winning percentage of .739.

THE FIRST GOLDEN ERA

Rolf "Chub" Poser came to UW from Columbus, Wisconsin, in 1932. He lettered three times in both basketball and baseball, serving as captain for the hoops team during both the 1933–1934 and 1934–1935 seasons. In 1935, he was the UW recipient of the Big Ten Medal of Honor for proficiency in scholarship and athletics. Poser was inducted into the UW Athletic Hall of Fame in 1993.

Arthur "Dynie" Mansfield is a UW sports icon who also played on the football and baseball teams and twice won university heavyweight boxing titles. After graduation, he joined UW's physical education department and taught for 36 years. He is a member of the UW Athletic Hall of Fame.

THE FIRST GOLDEN ERA

Harold E. "Bud" Foster served as head coach of the UW basketball team from 1934 to 1959. His 1940–1941 squad won the NCAA championship.

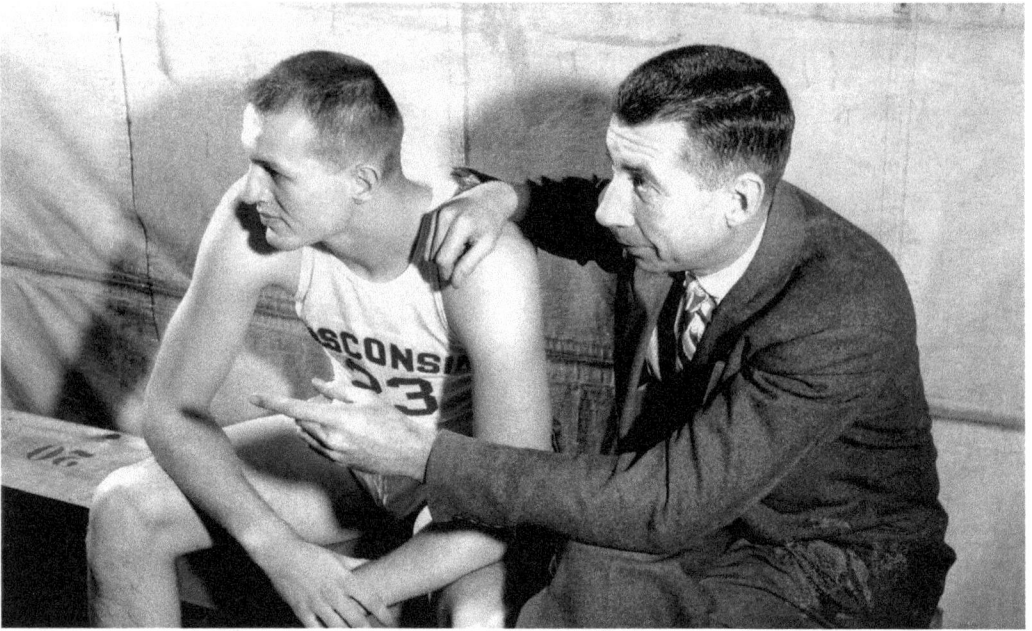

Harold E. "Bud" Foster became UW's freshman coach in 1933 and then took over the reigns as head coach the following season. He stayed on as head coach for 25 years.

Foster's career at UW includes being named an All-American center in 1930 plus coaching the team to the 1941 NCAA championship.

The 1934–1935 UW basketball squad finished the season tied with Purdue University and the University of Illinois for the Big Ten title. The Badgers won six of their final seven games, including a 37-27 overtime game versus Indiana University at the UW Field House. Two players from this team, Rolf "Chub" Poser and Gilly McDonald, were selected to the All–Big Ten team.

Fred "Fritz" Wagner was a member of the 1934–1935 Badger hoops team, which won 15 games and earned a share of the Big Ten title.

After playing basketball at UW, Fred "Fritz" Wagner served as a law professor at the university. He retired from the University of Wisconsin Law School in 1982. This photograph was taken around 1949.

Gene Englund served as captain of the 1940–1941 Big Ten and NCAA championship team. He was the leading scorer with 13 points in the Badgers' 39-34 victory over Washington State for the national crown. A native of Kenosha, Englund played center and was named All–Big Ten and All-American. He was a charter inductee into the UW Athletic Hall of Fame in 1991.

John Kotz twice received All-America honors while playing basketball at UW. As a sophomore, he was named MVP in the Badgers' 1941 NCAA championship game. In 1942, he led the Big Ten in scoring with 242 points during the 15-game season. From Rhinelander, Kotz was a charter inductee into the UW Athletic Hall of Fame in 1991.

Ted Strain (left) and Don Timmerman played on UW's 1941 NCAA championship team. In the Badgers' 39-34 win over Washington State for the national crown, Strain scored two free throws and Timmerman had one field goal.

HOOPS HISTORY

IN PROGRAMS

While reading through historic basketball game programs for research, I truly acquired an appreciation for how the sport has evolved. Take, for example, the official basketball program for the January 22, 1921, University of Illinois-UW game. Basketball could be a tough sport with boisterous fans during its early days, yet effort was being made to reduce this hardness. The back cover of this program proclaims in large print, "Let Us be Courteous to the Visiting Team and the Officials, and let us Abide by all decisions without Remark!" Inside, a good amount of copy is dedicated to further explaining rules for player and fan conduct. Under the headline "Home team responsible for conduct of spectators," it reads, "The referee shall call fouls on the home team for unsportsmanlike conduct on the part of the home audience. This includes objecting to the decisions of the officials or addressing remarks to them or to the visiting players." Then, when a player shot his free throw, "any attempt by the spectators or the opposing players to disconcert in any manner the player making the throw will result in a second trial given the player." Plus, the referee could offer the player additional free throws "in case the disturbance continues."

They did not call it the Roaring Twenties for nothing.

The Badgers moved from the Red Gym to the UW Field House in 1930. Even though UW had a tremendously successful basketball program for over 30 years at this point, many fans were still learning the game. The December 18, 1930, UW Field House Dedication Program features an article with the title "How to Watch a Basketball Game." It affected me as if I were reading profound ancient wisdom that remains not only relevant today, but worth dusting off and communicating once again. For example, "Observe the spirit of the teams in action, both with regard to their fellow members and to the officials. The smart coach will not permit his players to question decisions of the officials. Such conduct takes their minds off the game and gets them in the habit of looking for 'alibis' for their poor playing." I especially enjoyed this point: "Do not forget to give credit to a play well made, whether or not it is by the team for which you are rooting, or by the opponents. Such fairness tends to raise the entire tone of the contest and makes for better basketball and in the final analysis, a more enjoyable spectacle."

Regarding this last advice, I contend it is what Badger fans are known for to this day. An April 8, 2006, sports column in the *Boston Globe* written about UW hockey followers in particular, but all Badger athletics fans in general, stated, "It's great to see the enthusiasm and the positive energy they generate. . . . Imagine. Cheering for, rather than against. Think that could ever catch on in the East?" I live in New England and have gone to a few Red Sox vs. Yankees games at Fenway Park. Believe me, I know what he means. UW fans are wonderful.

Just like the great fans, UW's basketball programs through the years have reflected the fun game experience and shown respect for both the team's players and the coaches. Please enjoy some of my favorite programs on the following pages of this chapter.

Official Basketball Program

Illinois vs. Wisconsin

Saturday, January 22, 1921

Referee: Schommer   Umpire: Kearns

GAMES START PROMPTLY AT 7:30 P. M.

Michigan vs. Wisconsin

Monday, January 24, 1921

Referee: Birch   Umpire: Reynolds

University Gymnasium

NO ADMITTANCE WHILE THE GAME IS IN PROGRESS

SECOND SEMESTER SCHEDULE.
Northwestern at Madison—Feb. 12
Chicago at Madison—Feb. 26
Minnesota at Madison—March 5
Ohio State at Madison—March 8

ALL GAMES START PROMPTLY AT 7:30

This 1921 basketball program includes the January 22 game versus the University of Illinois and the January 24 match with the University of Michigan. The program's cover photograph shows basketball action inside UW's Red Gym. UW shared the Big Ten championship in 1921 with the University of Michigan and Purdue University. The Badgers beat the University of Michigan twice, but did not have Purdue University on their schedule during the season.

Captain Taylor

LINE-UP

Illinois	Wisconsin
Walquist, Forward	Taylor, Capt., Forward
Helstrom, Forward	R. Williams, Forward
Mee, Forward	
Reitsch, Center	Frogner, Center
Vail, Capt., Guard	
Collins, Guard	Caesar, Guard
Sabo, Guard	Tebell, Guard

Michigan	
Karpus, Capt., Forward	Knapp, Forward
Whitlock, Forward	J. Williams, Forward
Miller, Center	
Dunne, Center	Fanning, Center
Williams, Guard	
Rae, Guard	Horn, Guard
Williams, Guard	Frawley, Guard
	D. Reynolds, Manager

CONFERENCE STANDINGS

Jan. 17, 1921	Won	Lost
Indiana	3	0
Chicago	1	0
Purdue	1	0
Minnesota	1	0
Ohio State	1	1
Wisconsin	1	2
Northwestern	1	2
Iowa	0	1
Michigan	0	3
Illinois	0	0

Games start at 7:30 P. M. sharp—Be on time! No admittance after the game has started except between halves.

Caesar

All seats reserved for conference games. Ticket sales open two days in advance of game. Coupon holders must exchange for tickets before noon of the day of the game. Prices for conference games: 50c for end of court; 75c for end sections of the sides; $1.00 for center sections of the side seats.

J. Williams

GAMES THIS WEEK

Jan. 18—Chicago vs. Illinois

Jan. 21—Indiana vs. Minnesota

Jan. 22—Chicago vs. Iowa

Jan. 22—Purdue vs. Ohio State

Jan. 22—Michigan vs. Northwestern

Inside a 1921 UW basketball program, portraits of Badger players show the uniforms of the day. Line-ups are also provided; one name, Badger forward "R. Williams," refers to Rollie Williams, who also starred on the football and baseball teams and was named to the UW Athletic Hall of Fame in 1991. The Big Ten standings as of January 21 are also printed, showing UW's win-loss record at 1-3 before the squad made a winning run for the rest of the season to grab a share of the conference crown.

BASKETBALL INTERPRETATIONS

Home team responsible for conduct of spectators

The referee shall call fouls on the home team for unsportsmanlike conduct on the part of the home audience. This includes objecting to the decisions of the officials or addressing remarks to them or to the visiting players.

New Rule—A player may be removed from play and then returned once—providing he has not had four personal fouls called on him.

New Rule—A held ball within the free-throw lane shall be thrown up between two players on the free-throw line.

Free Throwing

In making a free throw the player is entitled to ten seconds for the throw after taking his position on the free-throw line. Any attempt by the spectators or by the opposing players to disconcert in any manner the player making the throw will result in a second trial being given to the player in case the basket is not made. The referee may continue to give the thrower additional trials in case the disturbance continues.

The Dribble

A player may dribble in any direction, in any way, and as long as he pleases until the ball comes to a rest, however slight, in one hand or is touched by both hands simultaneously when the dribble must stop and the ball must be passed or shot. The motion of the ball due to the bouncing or batting must be continuous. The player in starting the dribble may step one foot in any direction, but the rear or pivot foot must not leave the floor until the ball has left his hands. Standing still and bounding the ball constitutes a dribble. According to the new rules this year, a player who muffs or fumbles the ball can not start a dribble after recovering the ball, but must pass or shoot. A shot for goal is permitted at the end of a dribble.

Knapp

Jump Ball

On a so-called "Jump Ball," as when thrown up at center, or after a held ball, the jumpers must keep one hand behind the back and at the waist line until the ball is touched. On a jump-ball the ball must be tapped by either one or both players otherwise the ball is not in play and must be jumped again. Either jumper may catch the ball after it has been tapped which makes every man eligible to receive the ball after it has been tipped off.

Holding

Holding is personal contact with an opponent which in any way interferes with his freedom of movement. Usually called when a player hooks an opponent with bent arm or grasps the opponent or any part of his equipment in such a way as to keep him out of the play or from the ball. The majority of holding fouls, however, are made in guarding. When a player in guarding places both arms around an opponent even though both hands should be on the ball, constitutes a foul. This rule is largely misunderstood by spectators.

Blocking or Guarding

Blocking or charging, as when a player bumps an opponent out of the way constitutes a foul. A player may not interfere in any way with the progress of an opponent who has not the ball.

Fanning

A 1921 UW basketball program also featured a section with the title "Basketball Interpretations." This information shows how the game of basketball was still evolving. One of the new rules listed describes how a player leaving a game could later return "once, providing he has not had four personal fouls called on him." Before 1921, anytime a player was taken out he had to remain on the bench for the duration of the game. Another change to the game in 1921 was to move the backboards two feet off the wall. Backboards had been positioned on the wall, and so running up the pads underneath to shoot a basket had been a part of the game.

A ball hitting any edge of the back stop or its supports is out of bounds and goes to the opposing team out of bounds.

Disqualifications

A player is disqualified who has made four personal fouls. Personal fouls are held to include holding, blocking, tripping, charging or pushing, and any unnecessary roughness. A player may also be disqualified for using flagrant roughness on a player who is in the act of shooting a basket. Example, deliberately shoving a man in the back while shooting.

Extra Points

Two free throws are awarded when a player fouls an opponent who is in the act of throwing a basket. If the ball should be in the air and enter the basket the goal will count which will make possible four points on this particular play.

Call of Time

If the ball is in the air when the signal is given declaring time is up, the goal counts if ball enters the basket.

Tie Game

In case the score is tied at the expiration of the second half an additional playing period of five minutes will be called.

TICKET SALES

No reservations, no mail order, no telephone orders.

Coupon exchange for Northwestern game opens 10 A. M. Feb. 11.
Regular sale opens 10 A. M. Feb. 12.

Coupon exchange for Chicago game opens 10 A. M. Feb. 25.
Regular sale opens 10 A. M. Feb. 26.

Coupon exchange for Minnesota game opens 10 A. M. March 4.
Regular sale opens 10 A. M. March 5.

Coupon exchange for Ohio State game opens 10 A. M. March 7.
Regular sale opens 10 A. M. March 8.

Let Us be Courteous to the Visiting Team and the Officials, and let us Abide by all decisions without Remark!

Tebell   Frogner

College basketball games could be rough, boisterous events in the early days. By the 1920s, basketball programs described what was expected of the fans. On this page, next to a photograph of Badger guard and captain Gus Tebell (left), it states, "Let Us be Courteous to the Visiting Team and the Officials, and let us Abide by all decisions without Remark!"

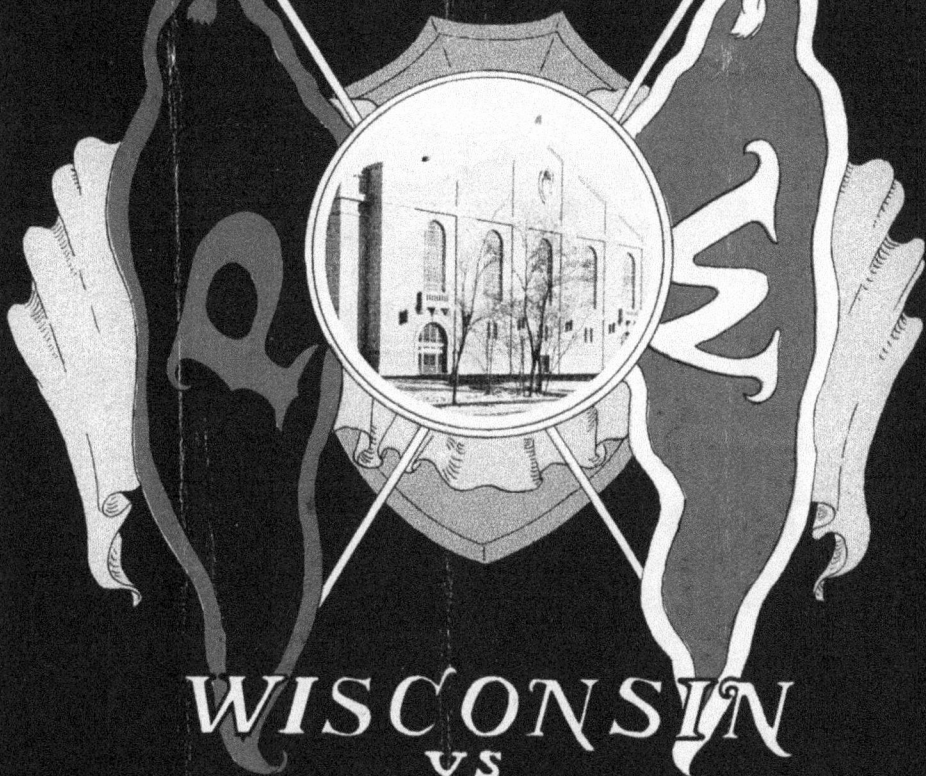

FIELD HOUSE
DEDICATION
DECEMBER 18, 1930

WISCONSIN
vs
PENNSYLVANIA

SOUVENIR PROGRAM   PRICE 25¢

This is the cover for the dedication of the new UW Field House on December 18, 1930. The Badgers defeated the University of Pennsylvania 25-12 for the inaugural game. A sellout crowd of 8,600 people was in attendance.

The December 18, 1930, UW Field House dedication program featured Badger players in action poses on page 5.

Congratulations to the University of Wisconsin on the completion of this wonderful new Field House

Also Welcome to the

New Park Hotel

200 Modern Rooms

1⁵⁰· Toilet and Lavatory **2**⁰⁰·

WALTER A. POCOCK
President and Manager

New Showers and Tub Baths **2**⁵⁰ up

Special Rates to Groups or Families

New Coffee Shop   *Cafe*   *Garage*

The Park Hotel has been thoroughly redecorated, refurnished and brought up to the last word in modern hotel service equipment at Popular Prices.

Dine at the Park Hotel before and after the Game.

Headquarters for all University, Prep and High Schools attending events in Madison—Special Rates.

Also

Hotel Frederic
St. Paul, Minn.

All Baths

$**1**⁷⁵ and $**2**⁰⁰

Finest Located Hotel in Madison

Madison   *Walter A. Pocock, Prop.*   Wisconsin

Madison's new Park Hotel bought an advertisement on the inside front cover of the 1930 UW Field House dedication program. Located across the street from the state capitol, the Park Hotel boasted itself as the "finest located hotel" in Madison. Rates ranged from $1.50 to $2.50 and up.

Third Annual

NATIONAL COLLEGIATE ATHLETIC ASSOCIATION

Regional Championship

BASKETBALL TOURNAMENT

at

The Wisconsin Field House
March 21 and 22, 1941

•

Team Entrants

Dartmouth College   **University of Wisconsin**
University of North Carolina
University of Pittsburgh

•

Price—10 Cents

For 10¢, a fan could purchase a program to the 1941 NCAA regional tournament in Madison. The UW hoops team first played Dartmouth College and won 51-50. The Badgers next defeated the University of Pittsburgh 36-30 to get into the national title game in Kansas City, Missouri, where they defeated Washington State 39-34. This famous team was led by National Basketball Hall of Fame coach Bud Foster and All-America players John Kotz and Gene Englund.

UNIVERSITY OF WISCONSIN BASKETBALL SQUAD

First row, left to right: Bob Alwin, John Kotz, Don Timmerman, Capt. Gene Englund, Charles Epperson, Ted Strain, Ed. Scheiwe. *Second row:* Coach Harold "Bud" Foster, Harlo Scott, Warren Schrage, Fred Rehm, Ted Deppe, John Lynch, Fred Wegner, Asst. Coach. *Back row:* Morris Bradley, Mgr., Ted Downs, Bob Roth, Bob Sullivan, George Affeldt, Ed. Jones, Trainer Walter Bakke.

University of Wisconsin Basketball Record, 1940-41

Wisconsin	39	Ripon	20	Wisconsin	40	Michigan	30
Wisconsin	38	Marquette	32	Wisconsin	44	Chicago	37
Wisconsin	44	Notre Dame	43	Wisconsin	46	Ohio State	31
Pittsburgh	36	Wisconsin	34	Wisconsin	59	Butler	55
Marquette	40	Wisconsin	30	Wisconsin	48	Northwestern	46
Wisconsin	52	Princeton	40	Wisconsin	46	Illinois	30
Wisconsin	46	Nebraska	31	Wisconsin	43	Purdue	42
Minnesota	44	Wisconsin	27	Wisconsin	65	Chicago	25
Wisconsin	49	Iowa	35	Wisconsin	38	Indiana	30
Wisconsin	48	Purdue	42	Wisconsin	42	Minnesota	32

Won 17, Lost 3

Wisconsin scored in conference games, 536 points (breaking former conference record of 519); conference opponents scored 424 points. In all games, Wisconsin scored 878; opponents, 721. Gene Englund won the "WGN" trophy as Big Ten's Most Valuable Player. Englund and Kotz named to Associated Press All-Conference team.

Page 3 of the 1941 NCAA regional tournament program featured a photograph of the UW basketball squad. Its 1940–1941 season record was also printed. In the copy at the base of the page, Gene Englund was acknowledged as the Big Ten MVP, and he and fellow Badger John Kotz were announced as Associated Press All-Conference team members.

WISCONSIN

VS.

LAWRENCE COLLEGE

AT

Wisconsin Field House

MADISON, WISCONSIN

MONDAY NIGHT, DEC. 2

●

SEASON'S SCHEDULE

Dec. 2—Lawrence at Madison*
. Dec. 7—Marquette at Madison*
Dec. 9—Butler at Indianapolis*
Dec. 14—Notre Dame at Madison*
Dec. 18—Oklahoma at Madison*
Dec. 21—Marquette at Milwaukee*
Dec. 23—Southern California at Madison*
Jan. 1—Illinois at Madison
Jan. 4—Iowa at Iowa City
Jan. 11—Indiana at Madison
Jan. 20—Michigan State at Lansing*
Jan. 25—Illinois at Champaign
Jan. 27—Northwestern at Madison
Feb. 3—Iowa at Madison
Feb. 8—Minnesota at Madison
Feb. 10—Michigan at Ann Arbor
Feb. 15—Northwestern at Evanston
Feb. 22—Ohio State at Madison
Feb. 24—Purdue at Lafayette
Mar. 1—Minnesota at Minneapolis

(*Non-conference games)

OFFICIAL BASKETBALL PROGRAM
Published by University of Wisconsin Athletic Department

PRICE 10c

On December 2, 1946, UW started its season by playing Lawrence College in Madison. For a dime, a fan could purchase this initial program of what would eventually turn out to be a superb season. The Badgers beat Lawrence 61-43 and went on to win the Big Ten title with a conference win-loss record of 9-3. Their 15-5 overall season record was strong enough to warrant an invitation to the NCAA tournament, where they lost in the first round of the East Regional to City College of New York by a score of 70-56. In the tournament's consolation match, UW then defeated the United States Naval Academy 50-49.

UNIVERSITY OF

WISCONSIN

WESTERN CONFERENCE CHAMPIONS

Wisconsin's varsity basketball squad gathers around the "W" in the Wisconsin fieldhouse. The players, first row, left to right, are Exner Menzel, Walt Lautenbach, Don Rehfeldt, Ed Mills, Bob Haarlow, Glen Selbo, and Bobby Cook. Second row, left to right, are Bob Krueger, Bob Mader, Tom Rippe, Doug Holcomb, Gil Hertz, Dick Falls, Larry Pokrzywinski, Doug Rogers, and Art Rizzi.

Basketball Season of 1946-1947
Madison, Wisconsin

●

Scores of All Games Played

Dec. 2, 1947—Wisconsin 61, Lawrence 43* (H)	Feb. 8, 1947—Wisconsin 60, Minnesota 51 (H)
Dec. 7, 1946—Wisconsin 65, Marquette 51* (H)	Feb. 10, 1947—Wisconsin 52, Michigan 51 (A)
Dec. 9, 1946—Wisconsin 60, Butler 52* (A)	Feb. 15, 1947—Wisconsin 54, Northwestern 42 (A)
Dec. 14, 1946—Wisconsin 53, Notre Dame 49* (H)	Feb. 22, 1947—Wisconsin 56, Ohio State 57 (H)
(overtime)	Feb. 24, 1947—Wisconsin 72, Purdue 60 (A)**
Dec. 18, 1946—Wisconsin 40, Oklahoma 56* (H)	Mar. 1, 1947—Wisconsin 55, Minnesota 58 (A)
Dec. 21, 1946—Wisconsin 47, Marquette 55* (A)	
Dec. 23, 1946—Wisconsin 61, So. California 56* (H)	*Non-conference games.
Jan. 1, 1947—Wisconsin 53, Illinois 47 (H)	**Game completed on Mar. 8 after Feb. 24 bleach-
Jan. 4, 1947—Wisconsin 63, Iowa 62 (A)	er crash at Purdue halted play when first half
Jan. 11, 1947—Wisconsin 70, Indiana 49 (H)	ended.
Jan. 20, 1947—Wisconsin 58, Michigan State 48* (A)	A—denotes game away from home.
Jan. 25, 1947—Wisconsin 37, Illinois 63 (A)	H—denotes home game.
Jan. 27, 1947—Wisconsin 45, Northwestern 44 (H)	Most Valuable Player . . . . . Glen Selbo
Feb. 3, 1947—Wisconsin 60, Iowa 53 (H)	Honorary Captain . . . . Walt Lautenbach

The 1946–1947 Badger Big Ten championship team was highlighted on the cover of this yearbook. The star players on this squad include leading scorer Bob Cook, wearing No. 22, and Big Ten MVP Glen Selbo, next to him with No. 21. No. 30, second from the left in the first row, is Walter Lautenbach, team captain and first-team All–Big Ten selection at guard. Seen third from the left in the first row, Don Rehfeldt would go on to be named Big Ten MVP in 1950 and, later that year, be drafted second overall in the NBA by the Baltimore Bullets.

UNIVERSITY OF

WISCONSIN
BASKETBALL SEASON OF 1951-52

Identification for cover picture—see page 7.

MICHIGAN GAME
WISCONSIN FIELD HOUSE

FEBRUARY 25, 1952   MADISON, WIS.

THIS PROGRAM PUBLISHED AND SOLD BY NATIONAL "W" CLUB
(An Alumni Organization of Major Letter Winners)

OFFICIAL PROGRAM — 15 CENTS

On February 25, 1952, UW hosted the University of Michigan, providing this program to fans for 15¢. The 1951–1952 season was not one of the Badgers' best, as they finished seventh overall in the Big Ten.

Charles Cable

Page 3 of the February 25, 1952, UW vs. University of Michigan program featured this full-page souvenir photograph of young Badgers star Richard W. (Dick) Cable. Below, he is inadvertently referred to as "Charles" Cable. He would go on to be the 1955 team captain and MVP and be drafted by the Milwaukee Hawks in the second round of the NBA draft. Cable was named to the UW Athletic Hall of Fame in 1998.

The back cover of this 1952 UW basketball program included a promotion for Oscar Mayer All-Meat Wieners. The Oscar Mayer Company, a strong supporter of UW athletics, advertised often in the sports programs throughout the years.

On January 19, 1953, UW played Ohio State in the UW Field House. Some UW basketball program covers, such as this one, opted for an artistic rendering rather than photography. In 1952, the UW football team won its first Big Ten title in 40 years and went on to the Rose Bowl, losing 7-0 to the University of Southern California. The 1952–1953 UW basketball team, however, was not as successful, finishing fifth in the Big Ten standings.

UNIVERSITY OF

WISCONSIN

BASKETBALL SEASON OF 1954-55

Western Michigan Game
WISCONSIN FIELD HOUSE
DECEMBER 6, 1954   MADISON. WIS.

THIS PROGRAM PUBLISHED AND SOLD
BY NATIONAL "W" CLUB
(An Alumni Organization of Major Letter Winners)

•

OFFICIAL PROGRAM — 15 CENTS

The program cover for the December 6, 1954, game between UW and Western Michigan University features a popular photograph set-up and location: team and coach gathering around the large W in the middle of the UW Field House basketball court. Coach Bud Foster kneels in the middle. The team's leading scorer that season, Dick Cable, appears at the far right. After graduation and a successful business career, Cable would return in 1995 to help the university as a volunteer fund-raiser for the Kohl Center.

WISCONSIN

BASKETBALL SEASON OF 1964-65

NORTHWESTERN

February 23, 1965   Wisconsin Fieldhouse

Official Program — 25ᶜ

PUBLISHED BY NATIONAL "W" CLUB
(An Alumni Organization of Letterwinners)

The February 23, 1965, game versus Northwestern University involved a program cover showing the entire Badger basketball squad. Coached by John Erickson, the team finished eighth in the Big Ten.

An advertisement from the American Dairy Association of Wisconsin in a 1965 program showed the collegiate style of the era and asked the reader to "drink 3 glasses [of milk] a day . . . the varsity way!!"

WISCONSIN BADGERS

BASKETBALL SEASON OF 1965-66
NEBRASKA

DECEMBER 1, 1965　　　　　**WISCONSIN FIELDHOUSE**

OFFICIAL PROGRAM — 25¢
PUBLISHED BY NATIONAL "W" CLUB
(An Alumni Organization of Letterwinners)

On the program cover for the December 1, 1965, game between UW and the University of Nebraska, Bucky Badger is in basketball action. This version of Bucky with a letter sweater was created in 1940 by artist Art Evans, but the UW mascot originally went by different names such as Bennie, Bernie, Bobby, Bouncey, and even Buddy. He officially became Bucky in 1949 after a contest to name the cheerleader gymnast, Bill Sagal, who wore a papier-mâché head of the mascot at football games. The winner was Buckingham U. Badger, or Bucky. The inspiration was a popular song urging the football players to "buck right through the line." Bucky Badger was almost replaced by a cow, Henrietta Holstein, in 1973 at the urging of state attorney general Howard Koop, but the effort failed.

"ROCK 'EM, BUCKY!"

In a 1965 UW basketball program, this advertisement from Nekoosa-Edwards Paper Company is a reflection of the times. A guitar-playing coed stands next to the pipe-smoking mascot under the headline "Rock 'Em, Bucky!"

The *Wisconsin State Journal* often advertised in UW's basketball programs. This 1965 program displays an artistic rendering of a shooting player next to the statement, "First in Sports Every Morning in the Sports Peach." This referred to a section of the newspaper with the latest sports news, photography, and scores.

This 1971–1972 UW basketball program shows a map of the Big Ten region with the faces of each head coach. Positioned over Madison is coach John Powless. His team tied for fifth in the conference that season.

BASKETBALL PREVIEW
1971-72

ASSISTANT COACHES

ASSISTANT COACH WILLIAM "BO" RYAN

On the same day that Coach Bill Cofield accepted the head coaching position at Wisconsin in 1976, he named William "Bo" Ryan of Chester, PA as an assistant to coach the guards.

The 31-year-old Ryan, who at the time was the basketball coach at Sun Valley High School in Sun Valley, Pa., had previously worked as an assistant to Cofield at the College of Racine in 1973-74.

Bo was a high-scoring guard for Wilkes College in Wilkes-Barre, Pa., for four years. He was captain and Most Valuable Player his senior year. Bo still holds two records at Wilkes—most points scored in a conference game (43) and most field goals in a single game (18). Coach Ryan was graduated with a degree in Business Administration in 1969 and later did post-graduate work at Villanova.

In 1975, Ryan was named Delaware County Coach of the Year as he guided the Sun Valley team to a 15-7 record and a second-place finish in the Philadelphia Suburban 2 League, despite having no starter over 6-1. The second-place finish qualified Sun Valley for the State Tournament for the first time ever.

Bo and his wife Kelly are parents of a daughter, Megan 4, and a son, William Francis 1.

This photograph of assistant coach William "Bo" Ryan was featured on page 9 of the February 23, 1980, basketball program for the UW–University of Minnesota game. Coach Ryan joined the Badgers in 1976 with a specific focus of working with the guards, but he would leave and later serve as head coach at the University of Wisconsin–Platteville from 1984 to 1999. While at Platteville, his teams would win 353 games while losing only 76 and capture four Division III national championships. Ryan then served as head coach at the University of Wisconsin–Milwaukee for two seasons, leading his teams to their first back-to-back winning seasons in eight years. He became the Badgers head coach in 2001.

WISCONSIN

Official Basketball Program
$2.00 Tax Incl.

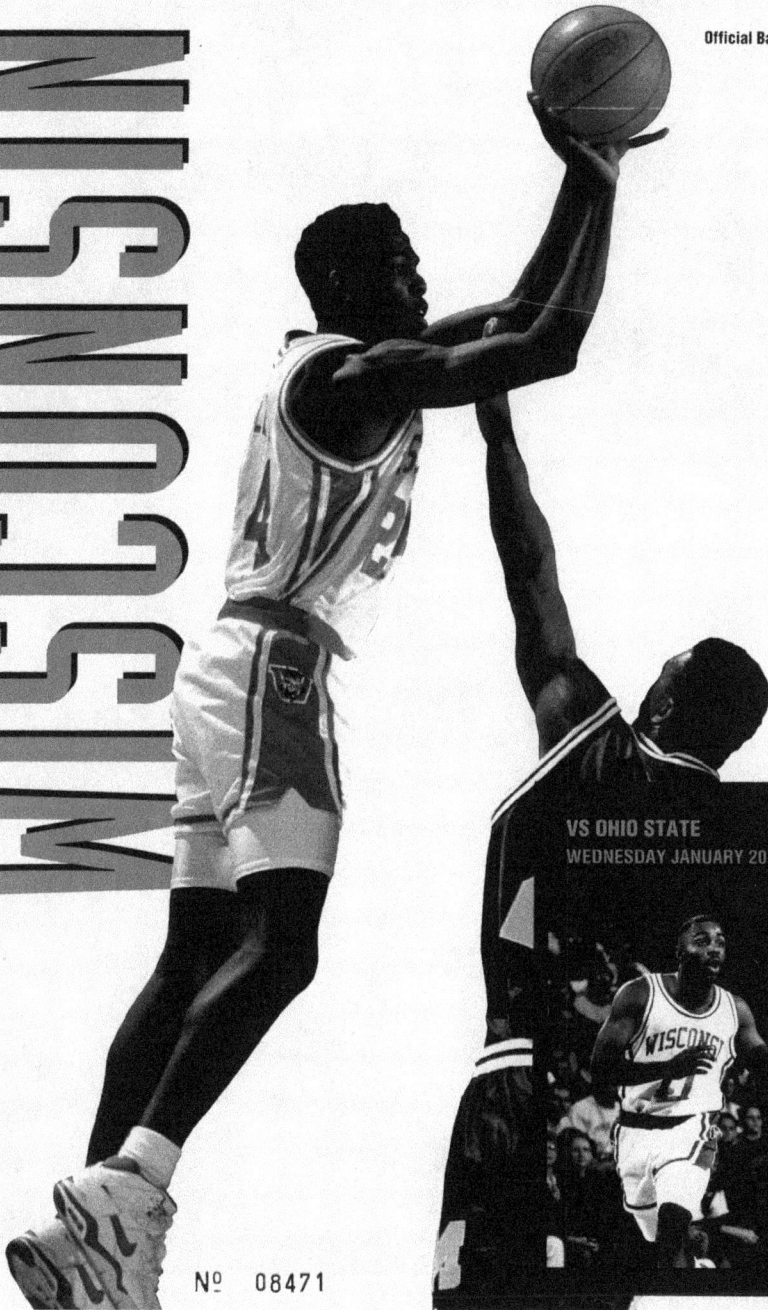

VS OHIO STATE
WEDNESDAY JANUARY 20, 1993

N⁰ 08471

Michael Finley graces the cover of the January 20, 1993, basketball program for a game versus Ohio State. A three-time honorable mention All-American, Finley's play at UW in the early 1990s rejuvenated UW basketball and helped launch the Second Golden Era in school history. Finley and teammates Tracy Webster and Rashard Griffith helped guide UW into the second round of the 1994 NCAA tournament. This was the school's first invitation into the NCAA postseason tournament in 47 years.

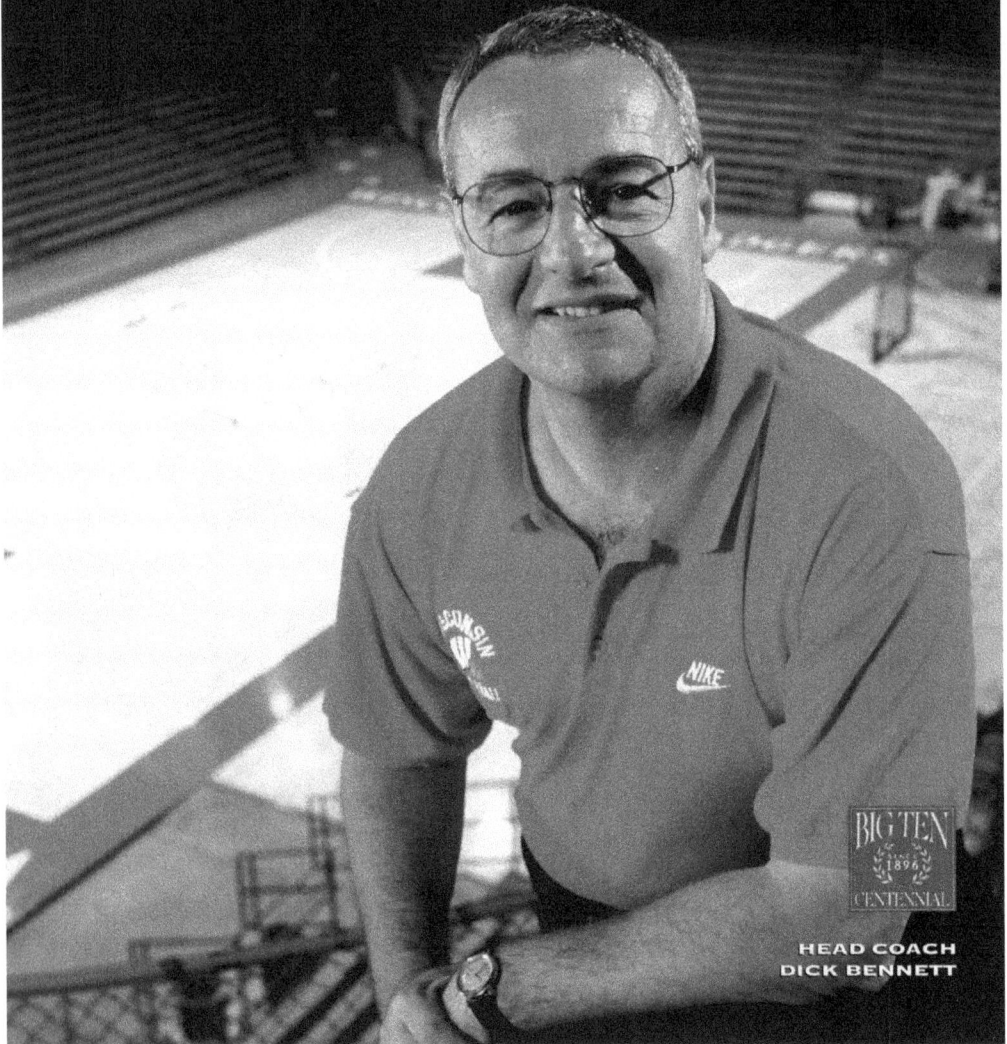

WISCONSIN MEN'S
BASKETBALL
1995-96 MEDIA GUIDE

HEAD COACH
DICK BENNETT

Dick Bennett appears on the cover of the 1995–1996 media guide for his first season as UW's head coach. The Badger hoops team finished eighth in the Big Ten race that season, but with a 17-15 overall record made it to the National Invitation Tournament (NIT). There UW defeated Manhattan College 55-42 in first-round play on March 13, 1996, but was then eliminated by Illinois State University 77-62 five days later. Coach Bennett would oversee many wins at UW, finishing in 2000 with his teams having won 96 games and losing only 69. During his five years as coach, the Badgers went to the NCAA tournament three times, making it to the Final Four in April 2000.

This program cover marked the last game at the UW Field House. Opened in 1930, the UW Field House could accommodate 11,500 fans and served as home for the Badger basketball teams through this final game versus Penn State on January 4, 1998. UW prevailed in this historic game, winning by a score of 76-57. After this date, all home games would be played in the Kohl Center with a seating capacity increase to 17,142.

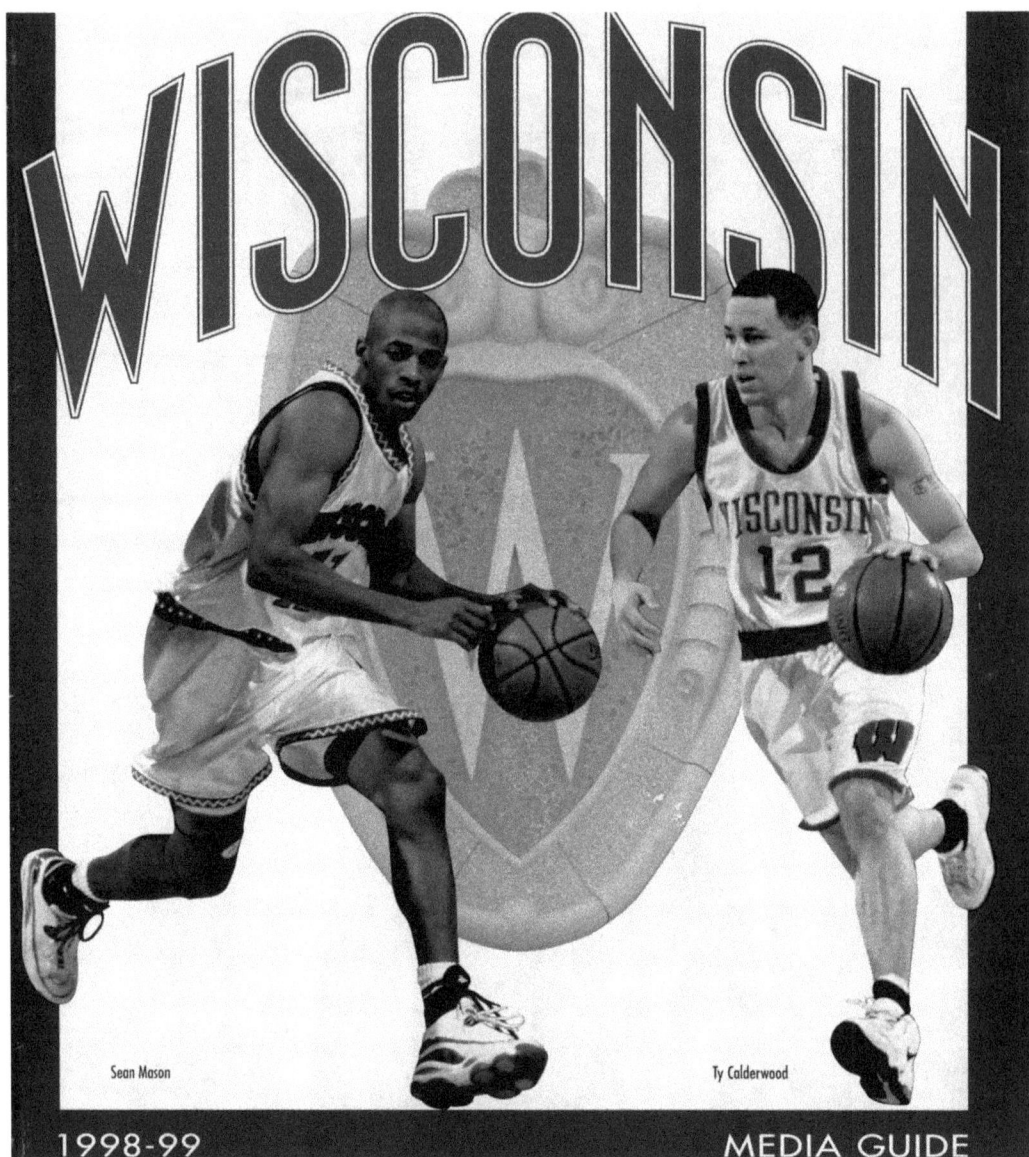

WISCONSIN

Sean Mason

Ty Calderwood

1998-99   MEDIA GUIDE

Badger hoops players Sean Mason and Ty Calderwood are pictured on the cover of the 1998–1999 media guide. This team, invited to the NCAA tournament, would lose in the first round 43-32 to Southwest Missouri State on March 12, 1999.

First-year head coach Bo Ryan

WISCONSIN

2001-02 BASKETBALL MEDIA GUIDE

William "Bo" Ryan was featured on the cover of the 2001–2002 media guide. Ryan came from the University of Wisconsin–Milwaukee to become the 15th head coach in Badger men's basketball history. On March 5, 2002, Ryan was named Big Ten Coach of the Year. UW made it once again to the NCAA tournament this season, defeated St. John's University 80-70 in its first game, but lost to the eventual national champion, the University of Maryland, by a score of 87-57 on March 17, 2002.

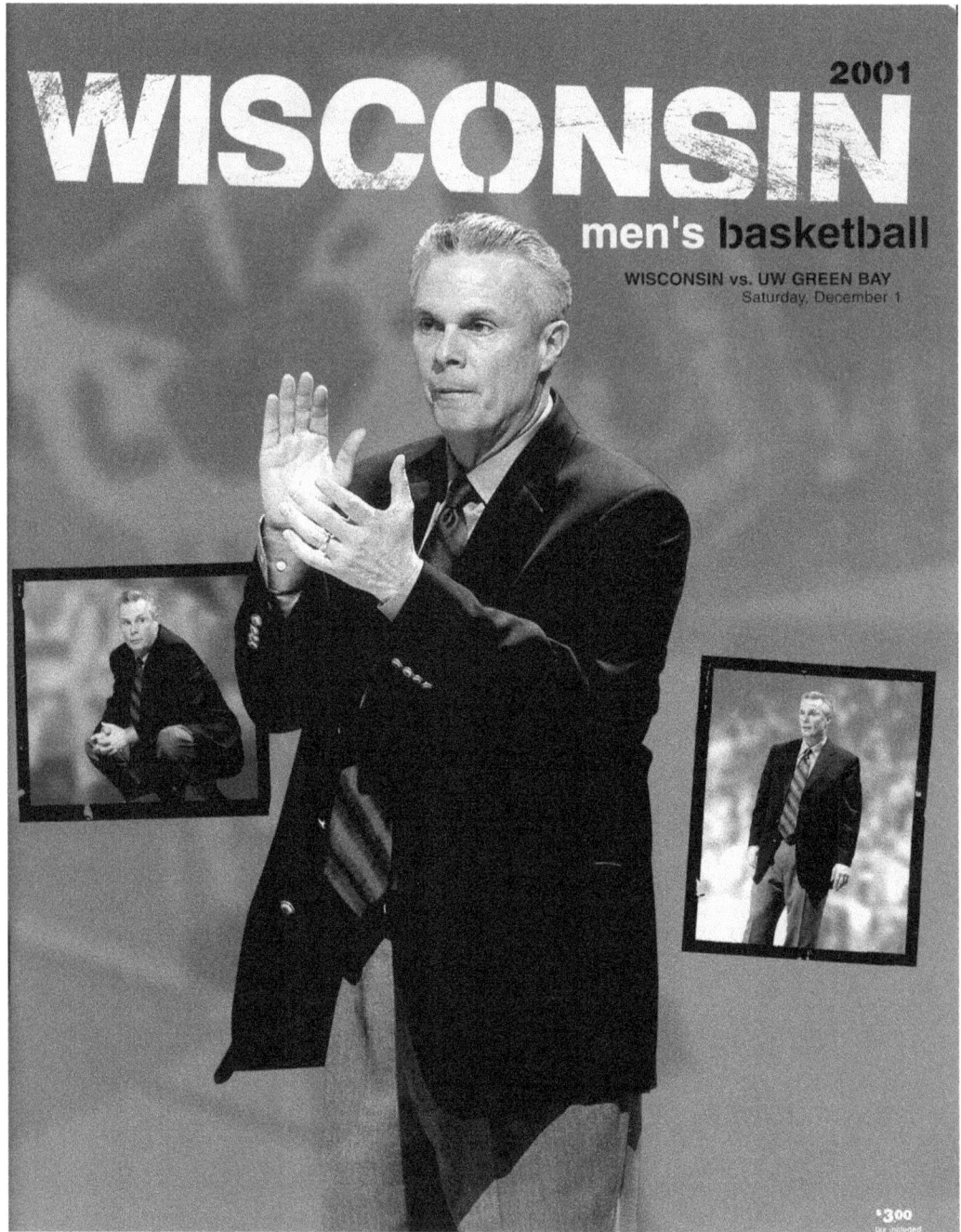

The December 1, 2001, program for the UW vs. University of Wisconsin–Green Bay game included three photographs of new head coach Bo Ryan. The Badgers won the game by a score of 70-57. This would prove to be a superb initial season for Ryan and his team as they earned a share of the Big Ten championship for the first time since 1947 and went on to the second round of the NCAA tournament.

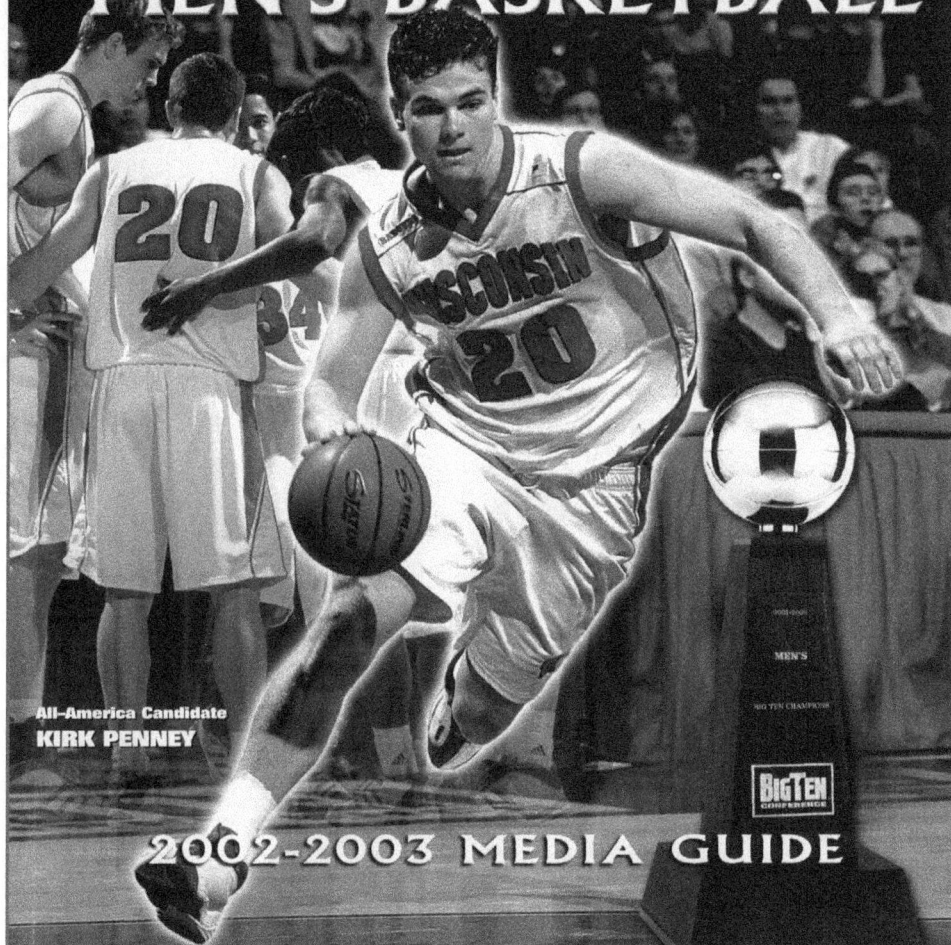

WISCONSIN

MEN'S BASKETBALL

All-America Candidate
KIRK PENNEY

2002-2003 MEDIA GUIDE

Kirk Penney graced the cover of the 2002–2003 UW basketball media guide. Penney would once again be a first-team All–Big Ten selection, the first Badger to be named two seasons in a row since Albert (Ab) Nicholas in 1951–1952. The 2002–2003 Badger squad would defeat the University of Illinois 60-59 on March 5, 2003, to win the Big Ten conference title. For the fifth consecutive year, this team would go on to the NCAA tournament, defeating Weber State 81-74 in the first round. The next game versus the University of Tulsa would see the Badgers down 58-45 with less than four minutes remaining, but they would go on a 16-2 run and prevail 61-60. Moving on to the Sweet Sixteen, UW eventually lost to the University of Kentucky 63-57 in front of 28,168 fans in the Minneapolis Metrodome.

The cover of the 2003–2004 UW men's basketball media guide featured players Alando Tucker, Dave Mader, Devin Harris, Mike Wilkinson, and Freddie Owens. Harris was named Big Ten Player of the Year on March 10, 2004, the first Badger hoops player to receive this honor since Don Rehfeldt in 1950. This team won the Big Ten tournament with a 70-53 victory over the University of Illinois, with Harris being presented the Outstanding Player Award plus earning All-Tournament Team honors with Wilkinson. This Badger squad also made it to the NCAA tournament, defeating the University of Richmond 76-54 in the first round, but lost to the University of Pittsburgh 59-55 in the next game.

3

THE RED GYM,
UW FIELD HOUSE,
AND KOHL CENTER

University of Wisconsin basketball home games have been played in three venues. The Red Gym, or "the armory," was built in 1892. Taking over in 1930 was the UW Field House. In 1998, the home facility torch was passed to the mighty Kohl Center.

The Red Gym still faces Langdon Street with its back to Lake Mendota. When the Badger men played hoops there at the beginning of the 20th century, it could accommodate 2,240 spectators. From what I can find, journalists covering games in the Red Gym were not extremely fond of it. One media description referred to it as "the little cigar box gym." In 1927, the *Daily Cardinal* reported that a Chicago newspaper contained a reference to the Red Gym as a "foul-smelling rat trap." Therefore it may sound odd that I, a UW student from 1974 to 1977, really liked the place.

During my college days, I saw the movie *The Paper Chase* in which Timothy Bottoms plays a Harvard student who swims ardently in his campus pool to deal with the stresses of college life. So when I felt some pressure during my student days in the early 1970s, I copied and became a swimmer as well. I did laps almost daily in the armory pool, wearing a Speedo faded to the manly color of pink and too-tight goggles that left oval indentations around my eyes for a half-hour after the workout. The breast stroke was my specialty because, well, I could not really do the other disciplines. Often I would dive deep pretending I was in the Caribbean or some similar clear, warm water. I had two reasons. One, it was a relaxing escape, especially when winter winds howled off Lake Mendota. And two, I hoped this might impress the bored, blonde student lifeguard sitting cross-legged in a folding chair on the far end of the deck.

My friends and I also played a lot of basketball in the Red Gym, and we frequently practiced there for our intramural team, Cancer Research. The team name choice was somewhat bizarre because none of us were in medical school or even premed at the time. We got it because our captain, Fred, did not have one in mind when he signed us up. When caught off-guard and asked at the intramural desk, he turned his gaze out the window and saw the McArdle Laboratory for Cancer Research building across the street. There you go. Despite the ambiguity, it was an honor to play for such a tremendous cause, and team Cancer Research did well, winning many games and almost, but not quite, the campus championship. On the court we called out to each other by our Kenosha hometown nicknames: Philly, D-Boy, Fal, Bud, McAdoo, Lars, Fred, and Bro-D.

Of course, at this time the real basketball on campus was performed by the varsity in the UW Field House. The dream to build the UW Field House commenced in 1925 with the hiring of George Little as UW's athletic director. By 1927, Little had put together a $3 million plan for replacing the Red Gym, the gymnasium annex, and the boathouse. An appropriation of $350,000 to begin was vetoed by Gov. Fred Zimmerman, so Little scaled back and turned to university regents. He received approval for just a new UW Field House, and on September 26, 1929, ground was broken on the southwest end of campus. Construction was swift. The building was dedicated on December 18, 1930, with a 27-12 Badger win over Pennsylvania before a sellout crowd of 8,600.

Enduring details placed on the UW Field House were the large W symbols located on the north and south sides. Over the years, many people have considered this crest to be the most beautiful UW symbol ever designed. Although it has become the university's official emblem, original field house architects Arthur Peabody and Paul Cret did not come up with it. The design was part of a contractor's bid in 1929, and the artist has never been identified.

When the $76.4 million Kohl Center opened in 1998 and UW basketball fans started to attend games there, a replication of the famous W from the UW Field House could be seen as they walked in the main entry.

The Kohl Center, named for Sen. Herb Kohl, who donated $25 million toward the project, stands off West Dayton Street on the southeast corner of the campus. Former UW basketball star Ab Nicholas and his wife, Nancy Johnson Nicholas, contributed $10 million toward the tremendous structure, and the adjacent practice facility was named the Nicholas-Johnson Pavilion. The Kohl Center holds 17,142 spectators (compare this to the 2,240 crammed into the Red Gym at the end of the 19th century). Over 40,000 cubic yards of concrete were used in construction, along with 30,000 square feet of glass. What is most important to Badger hoops fans, is that the Kohl Center has been a great place for the team to play. Case in point: a 38-game home winning streak took place until the number-one-ranked University of Illinois beat the Badgers during the 2004–2005 season.

From the Red Gym to the UW Field House and finally to the Kohl Center is quite an evolution. The following pages of this chapter feature some of the historic images along the way.

UW's Red Gym, or "the armory," is under construction on Langdon Street around 1890. It could hold 2,240 spectators for UW basketball games.

This photograph of the Red Gym was taken in the early 1890s from Francis Street.

Shown here around 1900 are the Red Gym and boathouse.

This 1907 postcard of the Red Gym was found while researching in UW's Steenbock Library. It bears an October 2, 1907, postmark and was mailed with a 1¢ stamp.

This is another early postcard of the Red Gym from the Steenbock Library collection. This time, the view is from Lake Mendota with the title *Boat House and Varsity Crew. Madison, Wis.* It was delivered with a 1¢ stamp in 1909.

This photograph was taken in the Red Gym during the UW vs. Ohio State game of 1917. The Badgers prevailed over the Buckeyes with a score of 40-15.

Various automobiles sit outside the Red Gym in this early view taken just across Langdon Street.

Members of the UW Athletic Board pose in front of the Red Gym before a basketball game versus the University of Minnesota.

The new UW Field House is under construction in 1929. The idea to build a new facility commenced in 1925 with the hiring of George Little as UW's athletic director. Little made moving UW basketball games out of the Red Gym a priority.

This image provides a close view of the UW Field House construction in 1929.

Shown here in a 1929 aerial view are the UW Field House construction and Camp Randall Stadium.

In this snowy 1930 image, the UW Field House remains under construction with a good amount of work to be done over the next few months. Dedication of the building would take place on December 18, 1930.

In the U.W. Field House Dedication Program of December 18, 1930, this historic photograph of the Red Gym was printed on page 21. The only text to accompany it was "The Old Gym—Passing from the Picture."

This early postcard shows the completed UW Field House and part of Camp Randall Stadium.

THE RED GYM, UW FIELD HOUSE, AND KOHL CENTER

WISCONSIN-MINNESOTA BASKETBALL GAME, MARCH 1, 1941
Won by Wisconsin, 42-32.   Attendance---13,750

On March 1, 1941, the Badgers defeated the University of Minnesota in the UW Field House by a score of 43-32. This team would go on to win the NCAA championship.

A 1960 Badger hoops game is played in the UW Field House.

THE RED GYM, UW FIELD HOUSE, AND KOHL CENTER

This photograph shows UW Field House second-half action on January 4, 1964, when Ohio State defeated UW 101-85.

The UW Field House and Camp Randall Stadium are pictured in 1970.

THE RED GYM, UW FIELD HOUSE, AND KOHL CENTER

The first game in the Kohl Center was played on January 17, 1998. The Badgers defeated Northwestern University 56-33 in front of 16,697 fans. One person in attendance was Sen. Herb Kohl, whose $25 million gift provided the primary funds for the $76.4 million structure.

The Kohl Center holds 17,142, a number that includes approximately 7,500 seats in the lower bowl and 4,500 in each of the two overhanging balconies. This special seating arrangement in the Kohl Center provides all spectators close proximity to the playing floor with excellent sight lines. The building's cantilever design is based on the overhang effect of the former UW Field House, but without the obstructions.

The Kohl Center is located on the southeast side of the UW campus. Over 40,000 cubic yards of concrete were used in its construction, along with 30,000 square feet of glass. When opponents are at center court and look up, they see three ascending spectator areas that are always packed with cheering Badger fans.

This *W* crest on the UW Field House was first seen in a 1929 contractor's bid. Although it has become UW's iconic symbol, replicated on the Kohl Center and seen throughout campus, the original artist has never been identified.

The *W* crest outside Gate A of the Kohl Center replicates the historic symbols on the UW Field House. In addition, all Kohl Center entry doors are adorned with the crest as well.

In 1952, UW basketball star guard Ab Nicholas was awarded second-team All-America recognition from *Look* magazine. Later in the 1990s, when plans commenced on the Kohl Center, Nicholas and his wife Nancy contributed $10 million toward the project. The adjacent Nicholas-Johnson Pavilion and Plaza and the Nicholas Suites were named for them. This photograph shows the beautiful memorial art on the Nicholas-Johnson Pavilion.

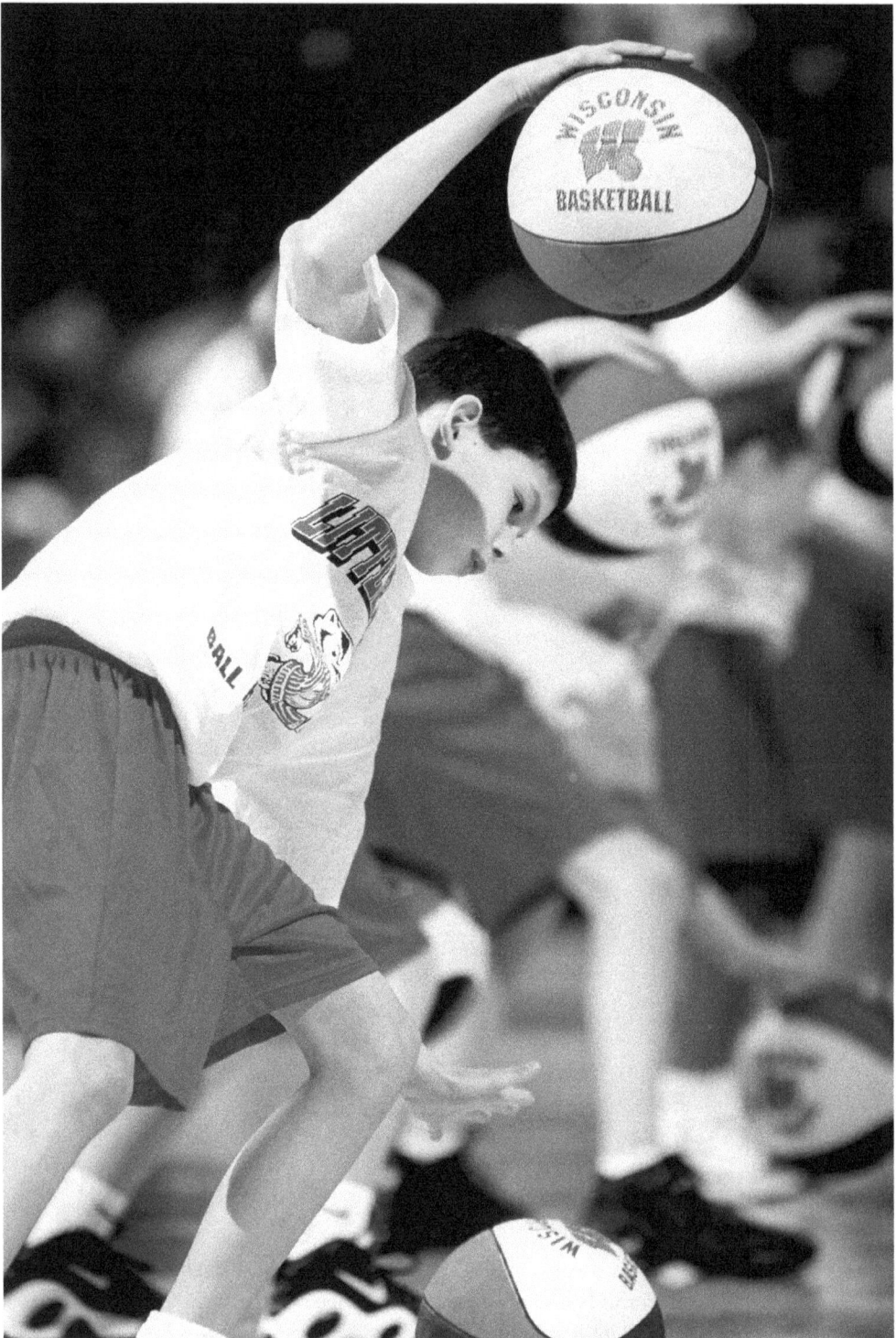

During halftime at a UW men's basketball game in 2001, little Badgers dribble on the Kohl Center court.

THE RED GYM, UW FIELD HOUSE, AND KOHL CENTER

4

Women's Basketball at University of Wisconsin

I was inspired to include UW women's basketball in this book after putting a Buddha in my yard and going on a bike ride, while my daughter Holly went skiing.

Allow me to explain.

During the month of April, the White Mountains of northern New Hampshire, where I live, may experience cold and snow, or swing extreme to a sunny and warm hint of spring. On this particular day, we welcomed the latter, although remnants of the former remained on the ski slopes of Loon Mountain, located just down the street—known as the Kancamangus Highway—from our house. So when Holly informed me that morning at the coffee pot that she would be joining her friends at Loon for a few runs, I told her it looks like a great day to do so—but be careful and do not forget to wear sunscreen. Parental message delivered, I next went into the garage and hoisted on a hand truck a life-sized statue of the meditating Buddha that had been carved from a tree trunk. I rolled and dragged him, with our feisty blonde Chihuahua and two knucklehead Australian shepherds barking along, across the wet and icy backyard to his garden perch. That rite of spring completed, I dressed warmly in my bike clothes, pedaled up toward the Kancamangus Pass, and thought about the history of sports in this country as they relate to women.

While doing research for this book, I found a wonderful photograph of the UW women's basketball team from 1897. That is one year before basketball officially became a men's school sport at UW. So the women were first? Well, not quite. Even though the women's hoops program got off to an early start in Madison, it was not as intercollegiate competition but rather play amongst interclass teams. It would take another 77 years before UW women's basketball would compete on a national collegiate level.

Title IX was the reason. This section of the Educational Amendment Act signed into law by Pres. Richard Nixon in 1972 was the single most important factor allowing for gains in women's sports in the United States. In its preamble, Title IX states, "No person in the United States shall, on the basis of sex, be excluded from participation in, be denied the benefits of, or be subject to discrimination under any educational programs or activity receiving federal financial assistance."

Chancellor Edwin Young appointed a committee to study athletics for women at UW in 1972 and 1973. The committee's recommendations asked for remodeling facilities and adjusting schedules to allow for women's sports participation on competitive teams, and also noncompetitive recreation. On March 1, 1974, the UW Athletic Board approved the addition of a 12-sport women's program. Partial scholarships were first provided to the women's basketball team in 1976. Then, in 1981, the Big Ten and NCAA recognized women's athletics with the sanctioning of conference and national championships.

The Kancamangus Highway—or "Kanc," as locals call it—was steep now, and I was wondering how far I would go on this first bike trek of the year. The Pemigewasset River sparkled under the morning sun with drifting remnants of ice to my right. There was hardly a car in sight. Big peaks towered ahead. I was breathing heavy and riding out of the saddle. When I made it to the hairpin parking lot, I was so happy I felt like getting off the bike and kissing the asphalt, but I did not. I just turned around and roared back down the Kanc, eventually catching sight of gray gondola cars and below it the white ribbons of snow that were Loon's ski trails.

I thought about Holly skiing there now and how she, her sister Isabella, and all American daughters of their generation received a greater opportunity to participate in school sports because of Title IX. My daughters have competed in basketball, baseball, and soccer, just like their brother David. I road back to the house and let the dogs out. This time they approached the Buddha calmly and rested in the warmth of the sun-kissed lawn in front of him, squinting and panting happily.

Spring symbolizes a fresh start. This Buddha sitting serene in the sunlight might say—if he could talk—that spring represents a chance to break out of a cycle altogether. It was a magnificent breakout change in the spring of 1974 when the UW Athletic Board added the women's basketball program. Please enjoy in this chapter some historic images showing the evolution of the very special women's basketball program at UW.

The first women's basketball team at UW is pictured about 1897.

This photograph of the freshman women's basketball team was taken in Ladies Hall, a facility built in 1870 to house the women enrolled in the university's Female College. Dr. Paul A. Chadbourne, UW president from 1867 to 1871, built Ladies Hall in 1871 because he believed women would be a distraction to the male students and therefore needed to live and study separately. In 1874, post-Chadbourne, education at UW was desegregated. In 1901, Dean Edward A. Birge renamed Ladies Hall in "honor" of Chadbourne (some information found while doing research indicated Birge chose the new name to "punish" Chadbourne for his opposition to coeducation). This original building was torn down in 1957 and replaced by the current Chadbourne Hall.

This women's basketball game was played at Lathrop Hall in 1916. The building was constructed by architect Arthur Peabody in 1910 when the university had 4,947 students (3,560 men and 1,387 women).

This historic photograph depicts a women's basketball game at UW in 1925.

The UW women's senior-class basketball team poses in 1927. Pictured here, from left to right, are (first row) Beatrice Thomas, Bernice Marion, Elizabeth Kuenzli, and Jo Winter; (second row) Rose Lander, Ernestine Long, and Ruth Will.

UW women's basketball action is captured in this 1935 photograph.

In 1984, Megan Scott participated on the basketball, volleyball, and track teams, becoming the first woman to letter in three sports at UW.

A Platteville native, Megan Scott was first in rebounding and third in scoring on the 1984 UW women's basketball team. Her father, Harlo, was a member of the 1941 NCAA championship UW basketball team.

This photograph shows the determined UW bench on February 21, 1992. In this game, UW defeated ninth-ranked Purdue with a score of 80-69.

WISCONSIN
Basketball

Senior
Dolly
Rademaker

UNIVERSITY OF WISCONSIN

WISCONSIN vs. MINNESOTA
UW Field House • March 8, 1994

This March 8, 1994, UW women's basketball program cover features Dolly Rademaker. A native of Thorp, Rademaker was an excellent three-point shooter for the Badgers and was also named All-Academic Big Ten from 1992 to 1994.

UW player Barb Franke is seen during a December 29, 1995, game versus Indiana University. In this season, the Badger women made it into the top 10 of the Associated Press ranking for the first time.

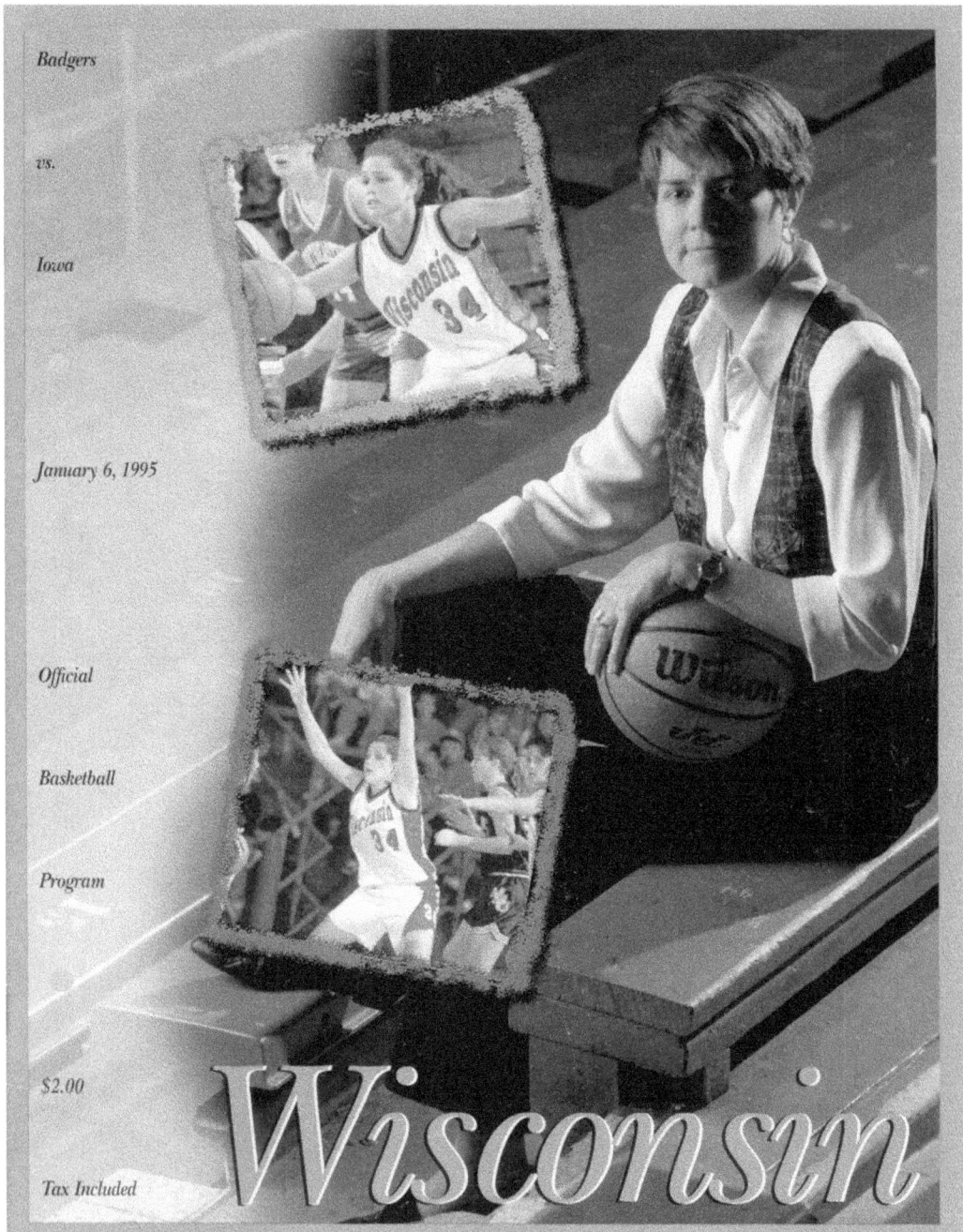

Badgers

vs.

Iowa

January 6, 1995

Official

Basketball

Program

$2.00

Tax Included

Wisconsin

Head coach Jane Albright-Dieterle graces the cover of the January 6, 1995, program for the UW women's game against the University of Iowa. Albright-Dieterle served as head coach from 1994 to 2003. Her teams posted an overall record of 161 wins against only 107 losses. In her nine seasons, UW went to the NCAA tournament five times and the NIT twice, winning the latter in 2000. Albright-Dieterle coached at a time when the UW women's basketball program became extremely successful and was popularly known nationwide as "BadgerBall."

The January 20, 2002, UW women's basketball game at the Kohl Center versus the University of Minnesota was sold out with 17,142 fans watching, setting a Big Ten record. UW ranks among the top schools in the nation for basketball game attendance.

Lisa Stone became head coach of the UW women's basketball team in 2003. She came from Drake University, where her 2002 team made it to the Sweet Sixteen of the NCAA tournament. In addition to winning games, Stone placed strong emphasis on her players doing well academically. Her 2004 Badger squad had seven members named Academic All–Big Ten. The 2005 team boasted four Academic All–Big Ten honorees. A native of Oregon, Wisconsin, Stone attended the University of Iowa from 1980 to 1984, where she played basketball and was twice named team MVP. In 1984, she was awarded the Big Ten Medal of Honor for being a top scholar-athlete.

This 2005 photograph shows an overhead view of UW coach Lisa Stone and her team at the Kohl Center.

A 2005 game at the Kohl Center featured the Badger women versus Michigan State. The 2005–2006 UW women's squad included sophomore Jolene Anderson, the fastest Badger player ever—male or female—to score 1,000 points.

5

FAMOUS BADGERS
IN BETWEEN
THE GOLDEN ERAS

If the Golden Eras for UW basketball were 1900 to 1941 and 1993 to the present, does that mean the years in between were "less than golden"? The honest answer is yes. I am certain there were many teams the Badgers played during this time who, when looking over their game schedules prior to the season, considered their upcoming contest versus UW a favorable match. For example, starting in 1980, the Bobby Knight–coached Indiana Hoosiers prevailed in 31 consecutive games against the Badgers.

As a UW student from 1973 to 1977, I recall some sorry hoops seasons. One friend from my hometown of Kenosha attending UW at the same time actually tried out for the varsity basketball squad—and made it. I do not recall him ever playing in a game but he did practice and travel with the team. He did have a nice shot. But that was in our campus intramural games, or when we played for beers on the outside court next to Ogg Hall.

There are two points I would like to make right now. One, this "In Between Era" is fortunately in the past. And two, even though the overall wins were not high during this time, there were some sensational players on the Badger men's basketball squads. Take, for example, Ray Patterson, who scored 738 points for the Badgers from 1942 to 1945 and was named an All-American. Patterson went on to participate in the NBA as a president and general manager for 20 years.

Bobby Cook's 1947 UW team became Big Ten champion, and Cook was the top scorer in the entire conference. The 1947 champs also included Walter Lautenbach, who lettered three times in both basketball and baseball and went on to play professionally for the Oshkosh All-Stars of the National Basketball League.

In 1950, Don Rehfeldt was named Big Ten MVP (it would be 54 years until another Badger, Devin Harris, would be named the conference player of the year) and first-team All-American for his play as center on the UW basketball team. After graduation he was drafted second overall by the Washington Bullets.

There was also Ab Nicholas. In addition to being a star basketball player at UW during the early 1950s, Nicholas served on the UW System's board of regents from 1987 to 1994. He and his wife, Nancy, donated $10 million toward funding the Kohl Center, the Badgers' state-of-the-art basketball and hockey facility that opened on January 17, 1998. Dick Cable starred for the UW basketball team from 1952 through 1955 and graduated as the Badgers' career scoring leader. In the 1990s, he volunteered as a fund-raiser to help the university with the Kohl Center project.

When many people think about UW in the late 1960s, student unrest and political activism come to mind more often than the basketball that was played in the UW Field House, so Joe Franklin might go unnoticed. Franklin was MVP of the 1967 and 1968 UW basketball squads. His 1,215 points and 858 rebounds over three seasons of play were UW records, and he was selected by the Milwaukee Bucks in the 1968 NBA draft.

Please enjoy the following historic photographs of some of the Badger basketball stars from this In Between Era. In chapter 7, entitled Badger Basketball Honors, I have also listed an array of player accomplishments and awards from all eras, 1898 to the present.

Ray Patterson came to UW from Beaver Dam and scored 738 points from 1942 to 1945. Named All-American by the *Chicago Herald*, he received All–Big Ten honors in 1944. Patterson was named team captain and MVP in 1944 and 1945.

After playing basketball at UW in the early 1940s, Ray Patterson went on to be president and part owner of the NBA's Milwaukee Bucks from 1969 to 1972. He also served as president and general manager of the NBA's Houston Rockets from 1972 through 1989. Patterson is in the UW Athletic Hall of Fame.

Bobby Cook was leading scorer for the 1947 Big Ten champion UW basketball team. He also led the Big Ten in scoring that year. He was named All–Big Ten as a forward twice, and his 847 points scored over three years set a UW record at the time. He is a member of the UW Athletic Hall of Fame.

Walter Lautenbach was captain of the 1947 Big Ten champion UW team. He lettered three times in both basketball and baseball while at the university. He was also named MVP of the 1943 baseball team. After graduation, he played for the Oshkosh All-Stars of the National Basketball League. He is in the UW Athletic Hall of Fame.

Guy Sundt not only played for the UW basketball team, but lettered in football and track. After graduation, he returned to the university to coach many sports, including the freshman basketball team. He served as UW's director of athletics from 1950 to 1955. This photograph was taken around 1950. Sundt is a member of the UW Athletic Hall of Fame.

Don Rehfeldt was named Big Ten MVP and first-team All-American in 1950 for his play as center on the UW basketball team. He scored 35 points in a 1950 contest against Northwestern University, a UW record that held up for 15 years.

A native of Chicago, Don Rehfeldt originally came to UW in 1944, but was soon after called into military service. He returned in 1947 and starred on the basketball team through 1950. He was chosen second overall in the 1950 NBA draft by the Baltimore Bullets. He is a member of the Illinois Basketball Coaches Hall of Fame and the UW Athletic Hall of Fame.

In the photo, on the player's jersey:

WISCONSIN
8

Text stamped on photo:

AB NICHOLAS – GUARD –1952
ALL BIG 10 – 1952
MOST VALUABLE PLAYER 51,5?

Ab Nicholas played for the UW basketball teams of the early 1950s. He scored 982 points in 66 games, a record at that time for a Badger guard. He was named twice to the first-team All–Big Ten, and in 1952 *Look* magazine honored him as a second-team All-American. Nicholas was inducted into the UW Athletic Hall of Fame in 1994.

Albert (Ab) Nicholas, UW star basketball guard during the early 1950s, received his bachelor degree in business in 1952 and a master of business administration in 1955. He and his wife, Nancy Johnson Nicholas, donated $10 million toward funding the Kohl Center. The Nicholas-Johnson Pavilion at the Kohl Center bears their family names.

Dick Cable starred for the UW basketball team from 1952 through 1955. After being named team captain, MVP, and UW's Big Ten Medal of Honor recipient in 1955, he graduated as the Badger's career scoring leader.

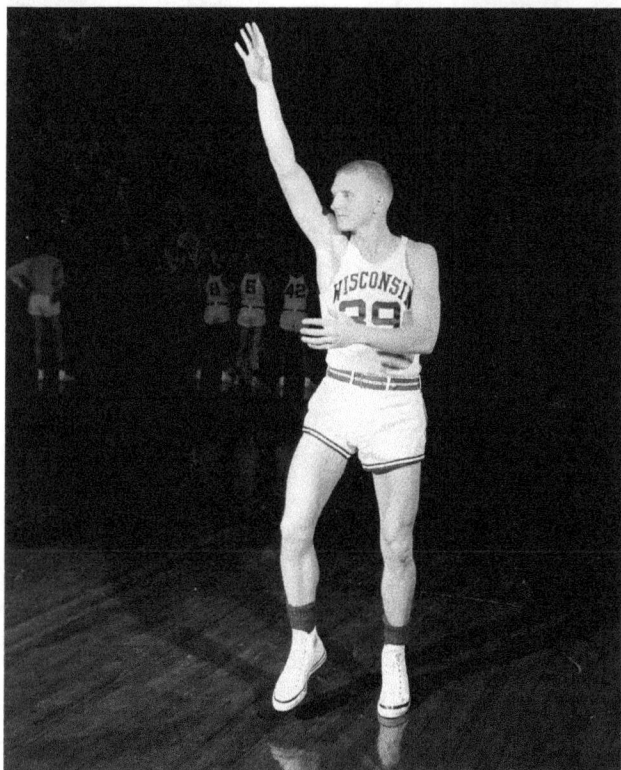

Badgers star Dick Cable was chosen by the Milwaukee Hawks in the second round of the 1955 NBA draft. He remained close to UW through the years, serving as a volunteer fund-raiser for the Kohl Center project during the mid-1990s. Cable was inducted into the UW Athletic Hall of Fame in 1998.

Joe Franklin was named MVP of the 1967 and 1968 UW basketball squads. He received first-team All–Big Ten honors in 1968. His 1,215 points and 858 rebounds over three seasons of play were UW records, and he was the 63rd player selected in the 1968 NBA draft, going to the Milwaukee Bucks. Franklin is in the UW Athletic Hall of Fame.

6

BADGER MEN AND WOMEN

IN THE POSTSEASON

Like most fans, I do not want to miss my team in the big game. For UW basketball, we are talking primarily about the postseason: the NCAA tourney. In 2003, when the Badger men played the University of Kentucky in the Midwest Regional of the NCAA, the game was held in Minneapolis. Simultaneously, due to my job in marketing requiring travel, I was 1,600 miles southeast in Orlando, Florida. No problem. Following the day's work at the Orlando Convention Center and a nice client dinner down the street on International Drive, I changed into my cardinal red T-shirt with "WISCONSIN" not so quietly printed on the front and drove to the big Ale House on Kirkman, where among the 30 televisions every NCAA game would be shown.

I entered and strolled through the crowds going from pod to pod of people, looking for the one watching the Badgers game. It took a few minutes, as the place was huge, but they identified me first due to my shirt. The Badger fans welcomed and adopted me into their group, the largest, happiest bunch in the place—UW fans always are—with a couple of waitresses buzzing among them, being kept busy.

UW had gotten to this point in the tournament—the Sweet Sixteen—by beating Weber State 81-74 and the University of Tulsa 61-60. Tonight versus the Midwest region's No. 1 seed, the University of Kentucky, it would unfortunately be a different story. I watched in dismay over the heads of our Badger contingent as the glowing screen claimed the Wildcats of Kentucky had prevailed 63-57. The Badgers had made it far into the prestigious NCAA tourney. All in all, it was a very good season, a strong performance. Our now-somber UW contingent could feel good about that. We collected ourselves, and a member of our group with a W on his hat led us all in a rendition of "Varsity."

Through 2006, the men's basketball team has been in the NCAA tournament 12 times. UW's overall NCAA record is 16-11. In 1941, they won it all, culminating a brilliant season (20 wins, 3 losses; the last 15 games were all UW victories) with a 39-34 victory over Washington State. The Badgers' NIT record is 3-4 with four appearances between 1989 and 1996.

The women's basketball program started in 1974. To date, the Badger women have participated in nine national postseason tournaments. They have been in the NCAA tournament six times (five appearances since 1995) with an overall record of 2-5. They are 1-1 with one 1982 appearance in the Association of Intercollegiate Athletics for Women (AIAW) national tournament. I have also included their superb Women's National Invitation Tournament (WNIT) history in this chapter. The Badger women have been in the WNIT twice, posting nine wins and only one loss. In 2000, they won the WNIT, defeating the University of Florida 75-74.

Overall, UW basketball teams have a 31-22 postseason (NCAA men, NIT, AIAW, NCAA women, and WNIT) record. This chapter describes in detail, featuring words and images, this postseason history.

University of Wisconsin Men's NCAA Tournament Results

All-time record: 16-11
Appearances: 12
Championships: 1 (1941)

1941
East Regional (Madison, WI)
University of Wisconsin 51, Dartmouth College 50
University of Wisconsin 36, University of Pittsburgh 30

NCAA Championship (Kansas City, MO)
University of Wisconsin 39, Washington State 34

1947
East Regional (New York, NY)
City College of New York 70, University of Wisconsin 56
University of Wisconsin 50, United States Naval Academy 49

1994
West Regional (Ogden, UT)
University of Wisconsin 80, University of Cincinnati 72
University of Missouri 109, University of Wisconsin 96

1997
East Regional (Pittsburgh, PA)
University of Texas 71, University of Wisconsin 58

1999
East Regional (Charlotte, NC)
Southwest Missouri State 43, University of Wisconsin 32

2000
West Regional (Salt Lake City, UT)
University of Wisconsin 66, Fresno State 56
University of Wisconsin 66, University of Arizona 59

West Regional (Albuquerque, NM)
University of Wisconsin 61, Louisiana State 48
University of Wisconsin 64, Purdue University 60

Final Four (Indianapolis, IN)
Michigan State 53, University of Wisconsin 41

2001

West Regional (Boise, ID)

Georgia State 50, University of Wisconsin 49

2002

East Regional (Washington, D.C.)

University of Wisconsin 80, St. John's University 70

University of Maryland 87, University of Wisconsin 57

2003

Midwest Regional (Spokane, WA)

University of Wisconsin 81, Weber State 74

University of Wisconsin 61, University of Tulsa 60

Midwest Regional (Minneapolis, MN)

University of Kentucky 63, University of Wisconsin 57

2004

East Rutherford Regional (Milwaukee, WI)

University of Wisconsin 76, University of Richmond 64

University of Pittsburgh 59, University of Wisconsin 55

2005

Syracuse Regional (Oklahoma City, OK)

University of Wisconsin 57, University of Northern Iowa 52

University of Wisconsin 71, Bucknell University 62

Syracuse Regional (Syracuse, NY)

University of Wisconsin 65, North Carolina State 56

University of North Carolina 88, University of Wisconsin 82

2006

Minneapolis Regional (Philadelphia, PA)

University of Arizona 94, University of Wisconsin 75

University of Wisconsin Men's NIT Results

All-time record: 3-4
Appearances: 4

1989
First Round (Madison, WI)
  University of Wisconsin 63, University of New Orleans 61

Second Round (Madison, WI)
  St. Louis University 73, University of Wisconsin 68

1991
First Round (Madison, WI)
  University of Wisconsin 87, Bowling Green State 79

Second Round (Madison, WI)
  Stanford University 80, University of Wisconsin 72

1993
First Round (Madison, WI)
  Rice University 77, University of Wisconsin 73

1996
First Round (Madison, WI)
  University of Wisconsin 55, Manhattan College 42

Second Round
  Illinois State 77, University of Wisconsin 62

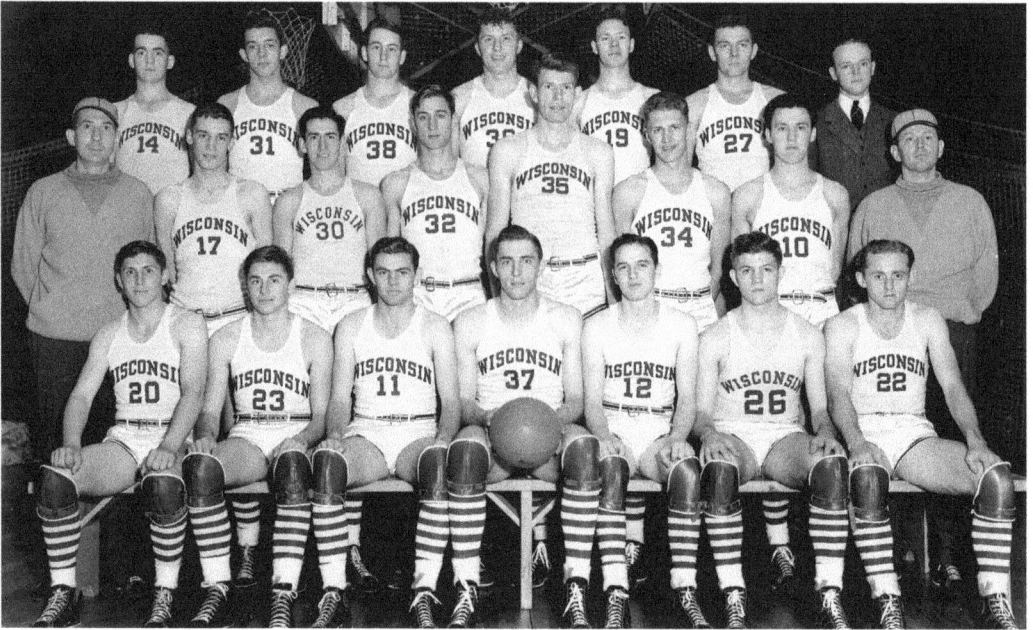

This UW team won the 1941 NCAA championship, defeating Washington State by the score of 39-34. The squad was coached by Bud Foster, pictured far left in the second row.

Basketball action occurs during the 1941 NCAA championship. The Badgers trailed Washington State early in the contest, but tournament MVP John Kotz would make two baskets to put UW ahead and ultimately win.

In the 1941 NCAA championship game, Gene Englund (left) led Badger scoring with 13 points. John Kotz (right) scored 12 points and was named tournament MVP. After the game, they posed with the trophy awarded to the No. 1 basketball team in the nation.

The 1946–1947 UW basketball squad returned to the NCAA tournament, receiving front-page coverage in the *Daily Cardinal* with the headline "Badgers Go On to New York." The Badgers received an invitation to the NCAA tournament after accomplishing a 15-5 season record and winning the Big Ten title.

Coach Bud Foster, pictured second from left, and UW captain Walter Lautenbach greet coach Nat Holman and two players of the Badgers' first-round 1947 NCAA opponent, the City College of New York, with an offer of Wisconsin cheddar cheese. The Badgers lost the game by the score of 70-56, but would prevail over The United States Naval Academy 50-49 in the consolation contest.

Michael Finley's career at UW in the early 1990s helped launch the Second Golden Era for the basketball program. Finley left UW as the university's all-time scoring leader with 2,147 points. He was chosen by the Phoenix Suns in the first round—21st overall—of the 1995 NBA draft. He would also play for the Dallas Mavericks starting in 1997 and be named an NBA All-Star in 2000 and 2001. As a member of the San Antonio Spurs in 2006, Finley played against Devin Harris—also a former Badgers star—of the Dallas Mavericks in the NBA playoffs. Michael Finley is in the UW Athletic Hall of Fame.

UNIVERSITY OF WISCONSIN BASKETBALL

After winning the NCAA championship in 1941, it would be 59 years until UW again made it among the final four teams of the tournament competition. In 2000, this rally with over 20,000 fans at Camp Randall Stadium honored the Badger men's basketball team for making it to the Final Four. UW defeated four teams—Fresno State, the University of Arizona, Louisiana State, and Purdue University—in NCAA tournament play to make it to the Final Four, where it lost to Michigan State by a score of 53-41.

This photograph shows Andy Kowske of the 2001 Badger basketball team in a game versus Penn State. UW won by a score of 63-58 and then went on to another NCAA tournament.

Coach Bo Ryan helps cut down the net in 2002 after UW clinches a share of its first Big Ten title since 1947 with a 74-54 win over the University of Michigan.

Fans celebrate on the Kohl Center court as the Badger men's basketball team clinches a share of the Big Ten title in 2002. With the victory, UW earned the No. 1 seed in the Big Ten tournament for the first time in school history.

BADGER MEN AND WOMEN IN THE POSTSEASON

UNIVERSITY OF WISCONSIN WOMEN'S NCAA TOURNAMENT RESULTS

All-time record: 2-6
Appearances: 6

1982
AIAW National Tournament (Austin, TX)
University of Wisconsin 60, University of Colorado 59
University of Texas 73, University of Wisconsin 61

1992
West Regional (Madison, WI)
University of Montana 85, University of Wisconsin 74

1995
Midwest Regional (Lubbock, TX)
University of Wisconsin 73, University of Kansas 72
Texas Tech 88, University of Wisconsin 65

1996
Mideast Regional (Nashville, TN)
University of Wisconsin 74, University of Oregon 60
Vanderbilt University 96, University of Wisconsin 82

1998
West Regional (Gainesville, FL)
Virginia Tech 75, University of Wisconsin 64

2001
East Regional (Athens, GA)
University of Missouri 71, University of Wisconsin 68

2002
Midwest Regional (Nashville, TN)
Arizona State 73, University of Wisconsin 70

University of Wisconsin Women's WNIT Results

All-time record: 9-1
Appearances: 2
Championships: 1 (2000)

1999
First Round (Madison, WI)
University of Wisconsin 80, Indiana State 43

Second Round (Madison, WI)
University of Wisconsin 107, Siena College 85

Quarterfinals (Madison, WI)
University of Wisconsin 70, Michigan State 69

Semifinals (Madison, WI)
University of Wisconsin 92, University of Memphis 73

Championship (Fayetteville, AR)
University of Arkansas 67, University of Wisconsin 64

2000
First Round (Madison, WI)
University of Wisconsin 83, Fairfield University 46

Second Round (Madison, WI)
University of Wisconsin 82, DePaul University 76

Quarterfinals (Madison, WI)
University of Wisconsin 77, Michigan State 45

Semifinals (Madison, WI)
University of Wisconsin 78, Colorado State 60

Championship (Madison, WI)
University of Wisconsin 75, University of Florida 74

The UW women's basketball team won the WNIT in 2000, defeating the University of Florida with a score of 75-74.

To win the WNIT in 2000, the Badger women had to defeat five teams: Fairfield University, DePaul University, Michigan State, Colorado State, and the University of Florida.

7

Badger

Basketball Honors

Men's Program

First-Team All-Americans
1905 Chris Steinmetz Sr.
1916 George Levis
1930 Harold Foster
1941 Gene Englund
1942 John Kotz
1950 Don Rehfeldt

John Wooden All-American
2004 Devin Harris

Helms Foundation Player of the Year
1905 Chris Steinmetz Sr.
1912 Otto Stangel
1916 George Levis
1918 William Chandler

Naismith Hall of Fame
(date is year of induction)
1959 Dr. Walter E. "Doc" Meanwell
1959 Harold Olsen
1959 Chris Steinmetz Sr.
1964 Bud Foster

NCAA Tournament MVP
1941 John Kotz

NCAA West Region MVP
2000 John Bryant

NCAA All-West Region
2000 Mike Kelley
2000 Andy Kowske

NCAA All-Syracuse Region
2005 Clayton Hanson
2005 Alando Tucker

Big Ten MVP
1941 Gene Englund
1942 John Kotz
1947 Glen Selbo
1950 Don Rehfeldt
2004 Devin Harris

Big Ten Tournament MVP
2004 Devin Harris

Big Ten Freshman of the Year
1996 Sam Okey

Big Ten Defensive Player of the Year
1999 Mike Kelley

World Basketball Championships
2002 Michael Finley (United States)
2002 Kirk Penney (New Zealand)

Olympics
2000 Kirk Penney (New Zealand)

Team USA
1993 Michael Finley

Goodwill Games
1994 Michael Finley

Badgers in the NBA
(date is year drafted)
*Denotes first-round selection
  1950 Don Rehfeldt, Baltimore*
  1952 Ab Nicholas, Milwaukee
  1954 Paul Morrow, Rochester
  1954 Rob Weisner, Milwaukee
  1955 Dick Cable, Milwaukee
  1956 Dick Miller, New York
  1963 Ken Siebel, Baltimore
  1963 Ron Jackson, Baltimore
  1964 Jack Brens, New York
  1966 Ken Barnes, Baltimore
  1968 Joe Franklin, Milwaukee
  1969 James Johnson, Boston
  1969 John Schell, Milwaukee
  1970 Albert Henry, Philadelphia*
  1971 Clarence Sherrod, Chicago
  1972 Gary Watson, Philadelphia
  1974 Kim Hughes, Buffalo
  1974 Kerry Hughes, Cleveland
  1976 Dale Koehler, Cleveland
  1976 Bob Johnson, Detroit
  1980 Wes Matthews, Washington*
  1980 Joe Chrnelich, New York
  1981 Claude Gregory, Washington
  1981 Larry Petty, Los Angeles
  1984 Cory Blackwell, Seattle
  1985 Scott Roth, San Antonio
  1986 Rick Olson, Houston
  1987 J. J. Weber, Milwaukee
  1995 Michael Finley, Phoenix*
  1995 Rashard Griffith, Milwaukee
  1997 Paul Grant, Minnesota
  2004 Devin Harris, Washington (traded to Dallas)*

Women's Program

UW Athletic Hall of Fame
(date is year of induction)
  1998 Barb Franke
  2005 Teresa Huff

Big Ten Freshman of the Year
  1988 Kay Fredrickson
  1992 Barb Franke
  1997 Kelley Paulus
  1998 LaTonya Sims
  1999 Jessie Stomke
  2005 Jolene Anderson

Big Ten Defensive Player of the Year
  2001 Tamara Moore

Badgers in the WNBA
  1999–2000 Robin Threatt, Seattle Storm
  1999–2000 Keisha Anderson, Washington Mystics
  2001–2002 Keisha Anderson, Charlotte Sting
  2002 Tamara Moore, Minnesota Lynx
  2003–2005 Tamara Moore, Phoenix Mercury

A UW basketball game breaks for halftime.

Visit us at
arcadiapublishing.com

....

www.ingramcontent.com/pod-product-compliance
Lightning Source LLC
Chambersburg PA
CBHW050605110426
42813CB00008B/2467